SO FN WHAT

Starting Over * Fresh & New
Wealthy, Healthy, Authentic & True

By G. L. Jenkins

Dedication

This book is dedicated to my parents:

Bert and Audrey Jenkins

Their unconditional love has enabled me
to become the woman I am today.

In fond memory of:

Jerry (Gerald) Keller

My childhood friend, who always believed in me and
encouraged me to finish this book!

Acknowledgements

I am immensely grateful for the encouragement and editing support that **Maribeth Jenkins Meeusen** provided. I don't think this book would have come to fruition without her outreach and offer to assist.

I would also like to thank **Robin Fuller** for her invaluable contribution to the editing of this book.

SO FN WHAT

Table of Contents

Section Four – It's a Wrap

SO FN WHAT

Starting Over * Fresh & New
Wealthy, Healthy, Authentic & True

Foreword

What a thrill it was to hear that Gail was writing a book! I've known her for over twenty years and watched her start over again in her life. It appeared to be effortless for her, although I know it wasn't. She writes from experience and gives you (step by step) what you can do to move forward in your life. Some of the information she shares is out there in other books, but the beauty of this book is that it is all in one place, and it is relayed in the context of her own experiences. That makes it a winner!

No matter what situation you find yourself in, be it ending a relationship and starting over, or it could be ending a job and starting over, or moving and starting over, or having health issues, Gail has gone through it. She gives many examples of how she moved through similar challenges. This book will help you move forward with some guidelines so that it doesn't have to be so difficult, confusing, or complex.

As we all know, many people fear the unknown and find it troublesome to move through change. Sometimes, all we need to know is that we are not the only ones. We can be inspired by hearing how others have gone through similar situations, and just knowing, we can use our own inner strength and courage to do the same. This book encourages you to do that.

Personally, I was going through some challenges of my own when I began reading her book, and believe me, it helped me to see more clearly what I needed to do.

This book is clearly written and is easy to read. She is not telling you what to do, she is sharing her experiences with you, and you can decide what might work for you, so that you too can create a rich and rewarding life after starting over.

Shelia Shumate
Sedona, AZ
Author of Divine Sparks and Cards
Motivational Speaker, Intuitive Counselor

Introduction

A few years ago, I entered the first phase of what would turn out to be a major life crisis. It involved a mystery illness, which led to a financial crisis, and then to a full-blown identity crisis. I honestly didn't think I would pull through it at the time. But one day, as I was paused in traffic in front of an assisted living facility, I began thinking about my own mortality. That's when something in me shifted. I became angry—really angry! I had what I refer to as my *"So FN What"* moment. That anger morphed into a determination that I could and would sort my life out again—no matter what!

My second shift came when I began utilizing some marketing and development techniques (from a past career) to get my life back on track. (Those techniques are included in this book!) Once I had successfully reestablished myself, I felt compelled to help others going through their own transitional periods in life.

Simply telling folks that they're going to pull through such times doesn't work. It sounds too pacifying and redundant at the time. I know; I've been there. But a book is something that people can pick up when they're ready and digest in small increments. That's why I wrote it. That's also how I designed it: to be received in small, manageable increments.

SO FN WHAT is about *starting over* again in life. Whether you chose to *start over*, or the Universe chose it for you, many of the processes and challenges will be the same. It is my sincere hope that this book will encourage you and serve as a substantive guide to help you through your own *starting over* transitions in life.

You'll notice that the book is written conversationally. That's because much of it was dictated and recorded while I was out walking. I decided to stay true to its original and casual format because I believe it presents a more natural and pleasant reading experience that way. It includes stories, anecdotes and encouragements. Each subject is designed to be its own essay, which can then be separated out and worked on as needed. You'll also notice that some of the concepts are italicized. That's because they're reprinted as notes in the final section, "It's a Wrap."

Below, I've included a brief outline of the book:

Section One – Starting Over: This section introduces you to some basic shifts in consciousness, which are simple to do and yet fundamental to the *starting over* process. They include telling a better story; understanding the power of gratitude; and responding to hope in such a way that your hope remains alive and strong.

Section Two – Fresh & New: This section discusses the challenges that arise when you seek to build a new and better life for yourself. It includes dealing with loss; the need for a period of discovery; how to push through resistance; and how to handle the saboteurs who show up and threaten to derail your perfectly achievable hopes and dreams.

Section Three – Wealthy, Healthy, Authentic & True: This section gets into the nitty-gritty of rebuilding your life. It seeks to redefine wealth by echoing Henry David Thoreau's eloquent assertion that "Wealth is the ability to fully experience life"; it goes over some tried-and-true practicalities for success (i.e., leadership, planning, understanding your money, presentation, critical thinking, and networking); it emphasizes the importance of maintaining your health; and finally, it introduces the concept that you are meant to be doing something special with your life—something you came into this world to do.

Also included in Section Three is the *Journey of Three Journeys*. The *Journey of Three Journeys* is a vision quest of sorts. It's something that you can engage in to connect with your higher power and gain more clarity on what you should be doing next in your life.

Section Four – It's a Wrap: This section is where all the italicized concepts have been gathered into notes, so that you can comb through them quickly and focus on what resonates with you. People don't like long reads these days, so this section is designed to be a kind of cheat sheet.

I believe that life is calling on you to engage in some new and genuine form of self-expression and service. I believe that's why you've come to this pivotal juncture in your life. I believe that you can answer this call and create something truly special for yourself, as well as thrive! I believe all of us can do this, as long as we are still here, lucid, and have the desire, understanding, and tools to do so.

Regardless of the circumstances that led you to it, *starting over* is always an opportunity to realign your life with more authenticity and purpose—ALWAYS!

—G. L. Jenkins

Section One:
Starting Over

Starting Over
Stories
Gratitude
Hope

Starting Over

Chapter One

I f you are *starting over* again, hitting the reset button at a later stage in life, YOU ARE NOT ALONE! Today, there are millions of us embarking on this very journey. We come from different socioeconomic backgrounds. We enter this transition through various circumstances—some are chosen—some are not.

If you are *starting over*, you are in for a grand adventure! Your life, and your role in life, are going to change exponentially. The road up ahead will present twists, turns, and directional changes that you can't even imagine right now. Whatever you create for yourself from here on out, it will be different from what it has been. And, it's going to be different from what you are imagining it will be. That much is certain.

It's a Quest

This starting over adventure, this quest, if you will, can be envisioned as a new and curious road stretching out ahead of you into the unknown.

Try to picture in your mind's eye that, high in the sky, centered directly above you, is a star. The star's purpose is to inspire you and draw you forward towards a more fulfilling and authentic life. The star is also a promise. It's a promise that there are real and tangible opportunities waiting for you ahead. It's a promise that you really can do something new and special with your life.

It's also a promise that, if you can resolve to move forward with a positive mindset and meet the challenges of this moment; and if you can apply the lessons and wisdom you've already gained through the years; and if you can embrace the concept that the Universe wants you to live an entirely different life with an entirely different set of rules; and if you can open yourself up to the new people and experiences that are poised and waiting to come into your life; then...

You will come to look back at this moment with great pride, because you're going to accomplish so much more than you think you can in this moment.

And, as you continue to walk down your new and curious road, in those inevitable moments of doubt, fear, and discouragement, try to also remember this:

Somewhere in the depths of your being, you wanted your contribution to this world to rise to a new level. That's what this time is all about. That's the call of the quest.

A Bit about Change

When we were young, we expected to be *starting over* in our lives. It happened to us all the time because our lives were constantly changing. We *started over* when we changed schools. We *started over* when we changed residences. We *started over* when we went to college, then again when we graduated. We *started over* when we got our first job, then again when we got a better one. We *started over* when we got married, bought our first home, and had our first child.

Life has always been about change and *starting over.* Right? Think about that for a moment. New beginnings have been the mile markers in your life. They're not just something you come to expect in youth yet shrink away from as you age.

You never want to settle too much on becoming too settled, because when you do, it becomes far too easy to slip into complacency. That's when you limit your ability to fully experience life.

You should seek to retain a degree of flexibility through-out your life, and especially as you age. Flexibility allows you to manage the ever-changing circumstances of life with more grace. Change is, after all, a natural component of life. Simply being alive in a living world means that you will have to navigate the challenges of change, however they come to you, for as long as you live.

Shifting Consciousness

If you want to move forward in your life, and go on to have many more meaningful and joyful experiences, then I'm going to suggest you try practicing some *shifts* in your consciousness that will help you to accomplish this.

Try *shifting* your thinking in times of discouragement, so you might instead *choose* to have faith that things can and will work out for the better. Try *shifting* your thinking in times of doubt, so that you might instead *choose* to have confidence in your decisions. Try *shifting* your thinking in times of pessimism, so that you might instead *choose* to be optimistic about your future. These shifts in consciousness are almost always choices. They rarely just happen on their own. Yet once you become adept at making them, then you will find yourself moving out of limited and fearful thinking and into a sense of self-empowerment instead.

Once you are able to shift into a consciousness of empowerment, versus a consciousness of fear and defeatism, then, given time, all change (even dreaded change) tends to realign into a more perfect order.

Youthful Wisdom

I think when we were younger, because our lives were constantly changing, we were more resilient to change. Even when unwanted change did occur, like the loss of a job, or home, or relationship, our youthful *change muscles* were well exercised and primed, and we tended to handle change with more fluidity. There may have been those all-encompassing, totally devastating moments when we thought our world was coming to an end, but we eventually worked through them and were able to move on with our lives. Well, what if I told you that, at least where the matter of change is concerned, your youthful self had it right all along?

Earlier I wrote, *"if you can apply the lessons and wisdom you've already gained through the years..."* When it comes to resilience, I want you to look back to your youthful self for those lessons and wisdom.

One of the great secrets of youth is that youthful energy is not stagnant. There is no status quo in a young life that lasts for very long. Youthful energy craves expansion. It's constantly creating and reinventing itself. Youthful energy inherently understands that a life that doesn't change doesn't expand. It doesn't grow.

If your life isn't growing and expanding, then either you're going to get the itch to change things, or the Universe is going to change things for you, or you're going to start to decline. There really are no other options.

The Good Ol' Days

For those of us who grew up in the fifties, sixties, seventies, and even stretching into the eighties, we can remember a time when *starting over* in midlife wasn't something our communities necessarily valued. Sure, there were those who reinvented themselves successfully and were seen as inspirational, but their stories were more often the exception than the rule. Back in the day, in most cases, when someone found themselves *starting over* in the second half of their life, they were said to be going through a midlife crisis, or it was assumed that some misfortune had befallen them, or that they had screwed up somehow. Either way, they were more likely to be judged or pitied than admired.

Well, you are no longer back in that day and that's *great* news! You are living in today's world, and you are going to take full advantage of the new opportunities that await you at every stage in life. Right!

Judgement

Turning away from those critical voices and out-of-date sentimentalities is a vital step you must be willing to take if you want to *start over* successfully in your life. Those judgements, whether they come from inside your own brain, or from your social or familial circle, rarely play a positive role in today's society, and they're not going to play a positive role in your life going forward either.

Negative mindsets have no place in this pivotal time in your life. You need to resolve, here and now, to shut them down and tune them out so that you can move forward with your God-given agenda and no one else's.

Making a fresh start in life isn't taboo anymore. And it's certainly not just for the young. *Starting over* has become commonplace in today's world. That's good news because fresh starts are actually healthy for us. They are energizing when embraced optimistically and planned out well enough. They keep life growing and moving forward in a positive trajectory, especially when you make it your intention that they do so.

People of all ages who bravely rise to the challenge of starting over, and are doing it well, are the ones leading rich and rewarding lives. They are the ones inspiring the rest of us and contributing to the greater good in our world, often in ways they never thought possible.

It's about Purpose

Trust me when I say that on the other side of this transition is a highly creative, capable person who stands squarely in his or her own energy and contributes to our world in a way that he or she is meant to be contributing.

Starting over is always an opportunity to realign your life with more authenticity and purpose.

It is my sincere hope that this book offers you some helpful suggestions. I hope it serves as one of those guiding stars in your sky. I hope it inspires you on your journey and encourages you to move forward with a little more grace and faith in your future.

Oh, and one other thing… Every time you *start over* under new circumstances, you have a chance to exercise parts of yourself that may have been stifled, repressed, ignored, minimized, or may have simply gone undeveloped.

Every time you start over in life, you have an opportunity to better harmonize what you do with who you are.

That's what this time is all about. That's the magic waiting to unfold. That's the *call of the quest.*

Stories

Chapter Two

Stories are sacred. They are existential in nature.

Every sentient being has a story. The entire human experience is a story. All the animals, plants, mountains, valleys, and rivers have their stories to tell. The earth, moon, sun, and stars have their stories as well. Even the Universe is unfolding in a vast and wondrous story.

Everything engaged in the expression of life has its story. And, each of us has the ability (if we so choose) to recognize and observe each other's stories—at least the parts we are privy to. Once we can do that, then we can't help but be amazed and respect one another more.

You too have your story.

As an individual, you were born either here or there; you developed this way or that; you've been challenged and shaped; you've loved, created, served, lost, mourned, struggled, overcome, failed, and triumphed. It all comes together and shifts like a living kaleidoscope until, in the end, you have your story.

We Can Change Our Stories

As human beings, we also have an ability for self-awareness. That means we have the ability to observe our own stories. That's a powerful gift because it means we can recognize, and then set out to change our stories when they don't resonate with who we are or want to be.

You won't always have control over what happens to or around you, but you will have control over how you respond, thus reclaiming power over your personal story.

You can always shift the narrative of your life story so that you step into better, stronger roles, versus allowing yourself to be completely defined by circumstances beyond your control. You can always reject and rewrite weak or floundering typecasting levied upon you by the outside world. You can always reject and rewrite undesirable typecasting levied upon you by your friends, family, and even yourself.

Telling a Better Story

I'm not talking about lying or pretending here. I'm talking about recasting yourself so that, starting today, you begin telling a better story about your life.

Are you always going to play the victim? Or would you rather step into the role of survivor? Or maybe even that of a brave advocate fighting for change? Are you going to go to your grave believing that you are unacceptable in some way, because someone somewhere made you feel that way? Or can you perhaps step into a better role of being accepting and comfortable with your genuine nature, knowing that you can be effective at achieving goals that are truly right for you? Have you lost some degree of independence, freedom, security, or health, and there ends your story? Or is there yet a better role for you to play in life? Perhaps one where you live a quality life regardless of your circumstances? Or maybe one where you lend support to others struggling with their own life-changing events?

Do you see where I'm going with this?

As long as you have self-awareness, you have an ability to tell a better story about your life and who you are in it, even in the grip of unfortunate circumstances. That's powerful stuff!

And here's the thing…

Once you begin telling a better story, and once you step into better roles for yourself, your energy shifts and life shifts with you. Circumstances start to change. The Universe begins to realign to support your new story because the Universe ultimately follows your direction.

When you begin telling a better story about who you are, you find yourself in a better story. It's that simple.

Far too few of us are aware of our ability to change our lives by changing our stories. Most feel powerless as they get tossed this way and that by events. While in truth...

You are far from powerless when it comes to your personal story because you always have choices. It's your choices that make you the ultimate narrator of your life.

The Day My Story Changed

A few years ago, when I was going through a particularly diffi-cult time, both physically and financially, I decided to go for a walk on a nearby hiking trail. I thought that by doing so, I might reclaim some of the joy and serenity I always experience when walking alone in nature. Only this time it didn't work. On this occasion, I was too depressed for the beauty of nature to penetrate my psyche. I was also in a lot of physical pain at the time. I was in the throes of a mystery illness that would take the medical community years to finally diagnose. My joints and muscles were so stiff and painful on this day that, with each step I took, pain seemed to reverberate along my skeleton until even my fingertips hurt.

Obviously, I didn't enjoy my hike. I couldn't even imag-ine a way out of my unfortunate set of circumstances at the time. I believed I was going to lose everything I loved and had built my life around. I knew I didn't have enough resources left (either physically or financially) to stop an inevitable downfall from happening, or even to rebuild with once everything did finally fall apart. It was a dismal chapter in my personal story, that's for sure. Perhaps my worst to date. I will never forget how all-encompassing my sense of dread was. I was way be-yond stressed out. I was growing numb and unresponsive as the weight of my hopelessness mixed with physical pain and crept into every aspect of my life.

I finished my hike almost as soon as I started it. I headed back to my car to drive home in somewhat of a daze. I fully expected to lose the house I was driving back to. I expected to lose everything. I even expected to die soon. That may seem overly dramatic in retrospect, but at the time, that's exactly where my consciousness was.

At some point during my drive home, I had to slow down and make a brief stop as the car in front of me slowed down to pull into The Sedona Winds, a nursing home just a few blocks away from my own house. There must have been something in that brief pause in traffic that brought about a pause in my despondent thinking as well, because I was able to stop thinking about myself long enough to consider this facility instead.

The Sedona Winds is a place where people go to live out their final days. I wondered what the residents there were like. Who had they been in their younger days? What were they most proud of when they looked back over their years? What were their regrets? What stories could they tell? I just knew that place had to be filled with stories—amazing stories about amazing people, times, places, and deeds! Stories certainly worth knowing.

That's when I had what I refer to as my "big epiphany." I saw my own life story, and I hated it! I mean, I really hated it! That's when something in me finally started to shift.

The Shift

One moment, I was wallowing in self-pity and thoughts of inevitable doom, and the next I was angry. Really angry! Like, defiantly angry! I was angry at myself! I was angry at my body! I was angry at life! I was even angry at God!

I saw my life spiraling downward and thought to myself, *No more!* I remember pounding my fists on the steering wheel of the car, hard, and saying something like, "No more! This is not going to be my story!"

I saw my life coming to an end, and me pretty much saying to my Creator (or even worse, my parents!), "Look, I got sick. Then I ran out of money. Then I gave up. Then I died."

Nope! That just wasn't going to happen! That was not going to be my story! No way, no how!

My life story might end up being that I was dealt some bad luck, but I hung in there and always gave it my best shot. Or it might be that I struggled somewhat, but always found a way to remain positive and tried to serve others in a positive way. Or it might even be that I went through some really tough times, only to pull through them and go on to succeed in some grand and wondrous fashion! But what it wasn't going to be was that I got sick, lost everything, gave up, and then died. That may have been my trajectory once, but no more!

My New Mantra (and it's not polite)

As traffic started moving again, I began brainstorming possible solutions to my many problems. That's when my so-called logical brain kicked in with its usual negative self-talk: *I can't do this because... That's not going to work because...*

My pessimistic mind tried its best to wrap me up (nice and tight) in no-win scenarios: *You're too sick to make enough money to accomplish what you want to accomplish, and you don't have enough money to go through the procedures you'll need to go through to figure out why you're sick. Soooo, this is it kid! It's over! You may have had a good run up until now, but this is the end of the road for you!*

Only this time, something was different. This time, a flicker of hope was starting to reestablish itself. My negative rationalizing wasn't reinforcing my negative mood the way it had been doing lately. Something in my energy was shifting. Just moments earlier, I had banged my fists on the steering wheel and expressed anger at God! That anger was still with me! I didn't feel defeated or depressed anymore, inasmuch as I still felt angry!

It didn't take long before *No more!* escalated into *So FN what!* And that's exactly what came out of my mouth as I sat in my car (now parked in my driveway), still tossing around worst-case scenarios in my head. "So FN what! So FN what! So FN what!"

Something in those words started to restore my energy. I think more so because I don't swear as a rule. *"So FN what!"* stoked my sensibilities in a way that was both provocative and defiant!

I found myself saying those words over and over again as I moved throughout my house. I said them when I kicked off my hiking boots, then again as I washed the dishes. My brain would start in with *I can't do that because...,* then out of my mouth would come, "So FN what! I'm doing it anyway!" *That won't work because...* "So FN what! I'll find a way!"

I once saw Tony Robbins give a motivational seminar where he taught the participants to punch the air with their fists whenever they were trying to accomplish something particularly difficult. I guess you could say that *"So FN what!"* became like my air punch. It became a sort of "Abracadabra!" against my pessimistic thinking.

It wasn't long before *"So FN what!"* became a personal mantra of sorts. I found myself saying it all the time in response to my negative thinking. I said it in response to others too (in my head of course, not actually out loud!) when they cast shade on my budding yet still fragile creative solutions. I said it to circumstances that threatened to derail my perfectly attainable hopes and plans. Whenever discouragement began to get the better of me, for whatever reason, from whatever source, it got the *"So FN what!"*

And, just like that, whatever was dragging me down at the time lost its tenacious grip and my optimism returned. My can-do spirit rekindled. I was no longer walking around like a zombie in my own apocalyptic story. I began making plans and mapping out potential solutions in a kind of *let's-throw-everything-against-the-wall-to-see-what-sticks* way! I started thinking in terms of my end game. That is, I wasn't so concerned with playing it safe anymore. I was more focused on what I could do today that my future self would be proud of for at least attempting.

On the Other Side

Today, thankfully, I'm on the other side of all that doom and gloom. Today, I'm living a much better life in a better story because I had the audacity to step into a better story.

Today, I'm enjoying relatively good health. It turned out I had a lupus flare-up, which subsequently attacked my thyroid, causing a secondary thyroid condition. And, although I did end up having to sell my house for financial reasons (something I hated doing at the time), it turned out to be the best thing for me in the long run. It didn't take long for me to find another beautiful home, which I ended up loving more than the one I had to give up! I went on to get my Arizona Real Estate License—something I don't think I would have done if I hadn't gone through a major life shake-up. Not only did that career choice prove to be viable (it certainly paid the bills and kept the lights on), but it also offered me a degree of flexibility, which made it easier for me to take care of my health. It also afforded me the time and resources to indulge in some of my more creative ideas—like writing a book!

Looking back, I shudder to think of how much time I wasted existing in a somewhat paralyzed state, all because of my limited thinking. I mean, come on… It wasn't like I wanted to be a ballerina on the moon or something. I wanted to be a relatively healthy, financially stable person living a happy, productive life and serving this world in some positive way. That's the story I wanted to live. What I wanted was never impossible. It was always possible!

SO FN WHAT

Which brings me to the title of this book: *SO FN WHAT*.

First of all, I want to apologize to anyone who is offended right now because of the suggested profanity. Trust me, I get it. But there is more to the title than just being incendiary.

As you've probably figured out by now, it's an acronym for the first three sections of this book: "Starting Over," "Fresh & New," and "Wealthy, Healthy, Authentic & True." But it also represents my own personal mantra of defiance—one that pushed back on all the doubts, fears, objections, and criticisms I struggled with when I was trying to turn my life around. That phrase, *"So FN what,"* is energetically defiant for me. It stops my obstructive thinking in its tracks. That phrase responds to my *oh-so-logical* yet negative self-talk by blasting right through it. That phrase responds to the *oh-so-wise-and-practical* objections of others by negating them without further consideration. That means that what's left are blank pages on which to write the story of my life my way, without all the negative programming.

Your Own Defiant Mantra

Make no mistake, when you are starting over in life, particular-ly when you are aspiring to create something authentic and true for yourself, you will have to tap into your defiant nature to make it happen.

You're going to run into many wonderful advocates and kindred spirits out there as you move forward on your *starting over* journey. Many will show up to encourage and support you. But there will also be others who will never understand what's truly right for you. They may seek to diminish your as-pirations in ways that are both overt and covert. Some may even mock you. You yourself may go through periods of self-doubt that could threaten to derail your perfectly attainable hopes and dreams, if you let them.

Unfortunately, that's because most of us have lived through years of conditioning that tells us the best way is the safe way, and the safe way is the status quo. It's a mentality you're going to run up against many times over. It's also a mentality you're going to have to learn how to shut down if you want to go on to accomplish something truly special for yourself.

That's where your defiant mantra comes in handy. It's a good tool to pull out of your proverbial toolbox whenever you need to give yourself that extra boost of resolve and tune out unnecessary negative feedback.

That said, you don't have to use my mantra. You can use it, but you don't have to. Feel free to come up with something of your own. Just make sure that for you, it's equally defiant. Make sure it's resolute. Make sure it shores up your resistance to pessimism and stokes the passions you will need to succeed. Make sure it effectively shuts down the disheartening criticism offered up by the outside world, as well as any limiting thinking going on inside of your own head.

Your mantra should never be spoken aloud to anyone. It's not meant to be offensive or to attack anyone. In fact, doing so will only create unnecessary contention, which will drain your emotional energy and divert your attention away from your better goals in life. No, the purpose of your mantra is to be your own secret weapon of defiance. It's the reason behind that mysterious twinkle in your eyes, indicating that you are stubbornly adhering to your own agenda, so that you might go on to accomplish whatever it is your spirit is longing for you to do.

Something Wonderful

Look, you are *starting over* in your life! You are on the edge of something wonderful, whether you know it right now or not. You are on the cusp of a better role in a better story. That's exciting stuff!

As you continue down your new and curious road, and as you continue to engage in your quest, try to remember this:

In order to live up to your potential, you can't pay too much heed to your limited thinking or the limited thinking of others. Dare to be defiant! Have a defiant mantra! Have the audacity to tell a better story, then step into that better role! Live that better life!

Gratitude

Chapter Three

When you are starting over in life, I can think of no better way to begin your journey than by consciously shifting into an attitude of gratitude. Regardless of your circumstances, there is always something to be grateful for—ALWAYS!

Gratitude is a force. In fact, I'm inclined to call it a superpower because, not only does it have the power to make you feel better at any given moment, it can transform the very nature of things.

When you shift your attention away from your struggles long enough to identify and give thanks for your blessings, you change your brain's chemistry; you change your body's chemistry; and you change your relationship with life itself.

This trifecta of change is like a magic elixir when it comes to creating a better life for yourself. Those who are able to do it through the power of gratitude, more often than not, go on to develop a more generous relationship with the Universe. They are the folks living rich and fulfilling lives. Whereas those who just can't seem to make that shift tend to find themselves in a more miserly relationship with the Universe. They are the ones who always seem to be at odds with the world around them, regardless of what they achieve or fail to achieve. And there's a reason for that…

While heartfelt gratitude is a pathway to a more harmonious relationship with the Universe, resentment and the lack of gratitude are pathways to a more conflicted relationship with the Universe.

It Supersedes Logic

When you stop to think about it, the power of gratitude seems logical enough, in that...

Graciousness begets optimism, and optimism is very attractive. It attracts more opportunities to you.

But the power of gratitude also seems to defy logic, in that...

Better opportunities seem to materialize out of thin air after you've sustained a state of genuine gratitude.

A Gracious Life

I was fortunate enough to have witnessed (during my formative years, no less) the profound momentum that gratitude gives to someone who is trying to build a better life for himself.

My father, Bert, was born in 1928 in Brownsville, Pennsylvania, just as the Great Depression hit. At that time, his father could only get part-time work as a coal miner, while his mother stayed at home and did her best to raise six children, including five boys and one girl. Together, they lived in a small wooden shell of a house owned by the coal company, with no electricity, and a wood-burning stove that sat cold more often than not.

My grandfather got paid in company tokens, which was not real money. That meant his family could only spend what he earned at the company store. That also meant there was no possible way they could save enough real money to try to prepare for a better future someday. The odds were certainly stacked against them. Their lives, deep in the mountains of western Pennsylvania, were harsh and dismal.

Then, in 1930, when my father was just two years old, his mother died twelve hours after giving birth to his youngest brother. She died in that cold, damp house in the still, dark hours of the morning without any medical care. Shortly after sunrise, the newborn baby was whisked away somewhere, and my father and his remaining siblings were taken to the county orphanage.

When Dad turned eighteen, he was drafted into the Army during the Korean War. After training at Fort Hood, Texas, his unit was shipped out overseas. One night, during a particularly fierce thunderstorm, the tent he was sleeping in got struck by lightning. That strike generated so much force that my father was ejected from his tent and landed some twenty feet or so away from it. As a result, nerves and muscles running along his right leg were damaged, causing him to have trouble with that leg for the rest of his life.

Yet despite his injury, I only heard Dad express gratitude for his time served in the Army. He used to say that it gave him a chance at a better life because it rescued him from an almost certain fate of working for either the local coal mines or steel mills (main employers in Appalachia at the time), neither of which he was too keen to do.

Once he was Stateside again, he married my mother, Audrey, and together they moved into a small apartment on Florida Avenue in Washington, DC. In the early years of their marriage, Mom chose to be a working gal by getting a job at Riggs National Bank, while Dad worked as a night watchman for The Hecht Company Warehouse.

I was still a toddler when Dad put himself through school and eventually earned his *"Certification in Electrical Engineering."* He went on to land a job with the International Brotherhood of Electrical Workers (the IBEW) in Washington, DC, and from that point on, he was able to provide a pretty good life for himself and his family.

The life that Dad built for himself was pretty much the quintessential American dream. He had his family. He owned his home. He had two nice cars in the driveway. He worked at a career he was proud of and excelled at as the years went by. It was all fairly normal stuff when you stop to think about it. Some might even say that his life leaned towards the mundane. But honestly, I don't think he ever thought of it that way. To Dad, everything he had was a blessing. You could just tell that's how he felt by the way he treated everyone and everything he cared for.

Every Friday night, for the rest of their lives together, Dad took my mother out to a nice restaurant. He attended every hokey elementary school and Sunday school performance I was in, and there were several of those a year. On weekends, when he had some time to himself, he liked to go into his workshop, turn on his transistor radio (always tuned to WMAL AM), and work on projects for the house or yard.

Growing up, I never once heard him complain about any part of our domestic life. He may have ranted on about politics or football, but he never made anyone in his life feel like they were deficient in any way. I guess he had lived through enough *bad* in his early years to know that normal life and family stuff wasn't it.

That didn't mean he didn't strive to improve his life. He did! He put himself through school. He worked his way up the ranks at the IBEW to retire as their chief engineer. He eventually moved his family into a beautiful new home in the pastoral countryside of Highland, Maryland. But even when he was preparing for bigger and better things, he always seemed to appreciate and care for what he had, for as long as it was there for him to appreciate and care for.

Dad lived a kind of charmed life as well. It was interesting to witness sometimes. If he was competing for a promotion at work, he'd get it. If he wanted a parking space close to the grocery store because it was cold and icy outside, there it would be, vacant and just waiting for him. Once, he even won thirty thousand dollars in the Maryland state lottery!

There was this common thing between us. Something unexpectedly good would happen, and I would say something like, "Wow, that was lucky!" And he would respond with, "Must be living right." He must have said those words to me a thousand times: "Must be living right."

But truth be told, Dad really was kind of lucky (even though he certainly wasn't born into luck). And he really was living right. It wasn't until years later that I came to understand just how often the two go hand in hand, and it's all related to gratitude.

Adding It to the Mix

Anyone, anytime, can enhance any aspect of their life by shifting into a state of gratitude. Gratitude changes things for the better the moment it's engaged.

Throughout my life, and probably because of the example set by my parents, I've been fairly good at recognizing and appreciating my blessings. But there have been those times when I lost the ability to do so. It was usually during especially difficult times, when I was so overcome by fear, disappointment, or discouragement, that my resting state of being became one of anxiety.

Getting through those dark nights of the soul took somewhat of a forced shift back into optimism. It also took some determination and planning. But whatever steps I took to improve or recover the floundering areas of my life, the effects were always bolstered once I remembered to shift back into a state of gratitude. Time and time again, this has proved to be the case.

Regardless of what you are going through, you can always improve your personal energy, as well as your circumstances, by recognizing and giving thanks for your blessings.

Expressing Gratitude

Expressions of gratitude can be spoken, certainly, but there are other ways to express gratitude.

It is really through a combination of acknowledgement, enjoyment, and care that you demonstrate to the Universe you are truly grateful.

Ways to Express Gratitude

Acknowledgement – Acknowledging what you are grateful for in life is the first and easiest step you can take to move into a state of gratitude. Acknowledgement is that pause you take to simply note your blessings. Acknowledgement can be spoken aloud or expressed privately in thought or prayer.

My favorite time of day to acknowledge my blessings is first thing in the morning while having my coffee. I like to sit cross-legged on the couch and reflect on what I'm thankful for, like my family, friends, pets, home… or even the way the morning light slips through the blinds, promising yet another day on planet Earth. In this way, gratitude sets my day.

Enjoyment – Enjoyment is another way to express gratitude. Enjoyment requires your presence. Taking time out of a task-driven day to simply enjoy your experience with someone or something demonstrates that you are grateful for them.

Enjoying your spouse's company at his or her favorite restaurant, or going for a walk on a particularly gorgeous day—both are expressions of gratitude.

Care – When you tend to the people and things in your life, or when you take care of your business, employees, customers, home, car, pets, or anything else that you have been blessed with, your caring actions are like animated prayers of gratitude.

When you provide for your family, check in on a friend, send a greeting card, or even when you're careful not to unnecessarily damage the environment, you demonstrate to the Universe that these people, places, and things are important to you.

Think of it this way: when you give someone a gift, could the way they acknowledge, enjoy, and care for that gift affect how you give to them in the future?

Make no mistake, we are each in a personal relationship with the Universe. Therefore, remember to nurture that relationship by acknowledging, enjoying, and caring for her gifts.

Life Is Both Joy and Pain

Life isn't always going to be easy. You will experience much joy in this lifetime, but you will experience heartbreaking pain and strife as well. No one escapes the painful bits.

Everything is changing. People, places, and situations are constantly passing in and out of your life, whether you want them to or not. All of this takes its toll on your heart and mind. Nevertheless, you are still the narrator of your own life, because it is what you choose to focus on that will ultimately define you.

Looking back over my father's story, I realize he could have focused on the many hardships and injustices in his life. There certainly were enough of them—many more than I've touched upon in this book. But Dad had this beautiful ability to shift his focus back onto what was there for him to appreciate in the moment, and then direct his love and gratitude there. He acknowledged, enjoyed, and cared for the many gifts in his life. I personally believe it was his propensity for gratitude that helped heal much of the trauma from his past and fuel his optimism for life. His relationship with the Universe was a good one and, as such, the overall story of his life was that of a loving and gracious man who was ultimately loved and graced.

You may have to overcome any number of hardships and losses as you seek to rebuild your life. Remembering to express gratitude is yet another tool you can use to get through the more challenging times. Once engaged, gratitude changes the reality of things for the better.

Hope

Chapter Four

In the last dark moments of night, when the eastern sky begins to glow with a faint hint of dawn, there too rises hope. When a newborn child is placed into his mother's arms, and then cradled to her breasts for the first time, there too rests hope. When one chapter in life closes and another opens, still blank and veiled in mystery, there too awaits hope. Where there are endings, there are beginnings. Where there are beginnings, there is hope.

Emily Dickinson wrote of hope,

"Hope is the thing with feathers, that perches in the soul…"

Hope is indeed a light and airy spirit that rests within each of us, awaiting its moment to rise. Hope offers us no burden to bear because its purpose in our lives is to lift our mood and lighten our burdens.

Nothing that lives, thrives without hope. Without hope, life draws inward and begins to wither.

You're Not Always Going to Feel It

There is another aspect to hope, however, that's worth noting: you're not always going to feel it. Sometimes, that thing with feathers seems to up and fly away.

Having hope at the beginning of any project is beyond important. You're just not going to accomplish much without it. But you're not always going to feel hopeful either—not from start to finish.

There is another quote by J. R. R. Tolkien (from *The Fellowship of the Ring*) that rings equally true. When the road up ahead appears particularly bleak, sometimes...

"We must do without hope." —Aragorn

That sentiment, *"We must do without hope,"* resonates with me, because the one thing in life I have trouble doing is moving forward when I don't feel particularly hopeful in the moment.

I function primarily out of my right brain, which means that feelings are fundamental to how I operate. It also means that discouragement, or the absence of feeling hopeful in any given moment, can stop me in my tracks. I have dropped the ball on so many worthwhile projects because things got too tangled, or too difficult, then I got discouraged, then I lost hope, and then momentum. Understanding that I could and should continue to move forward with my plans, without always feeling hopeful, has been a monumental life lesson for me.

Hope ebbs and wanes as circumstances shift and change. Regardless, we must remain committed to moving forward in our lives.

Feeding Hope

A few years ago, when I was driving through the mountains to visit a friend in Romney, West Virginia, my jazzy radio station started to cut out and a local religious station began to overpower its airspace. I was just about to change the station when I caught a snippet from a pastor's sermon about our ability to *feed* hope. I hesitated for a moment, then changed the station. But the concept that I can intentionally feed my hope has stuck with me through the years.

Over time, and after going through my own struggles in life, I have come to understand that hope doesn't have to be some autonomous thing that comes and goes at will. That pastor's sermon, all those years ago, was right on. We, as human beings, can intentionally feed our hope. We can nurture and give back to hope in such a way that our capacity for hope remains strong.

A Relationship with Hope

You are, in fact, in a relationship with hope. And just as in all relationships, you strengthen that relationship by responding to it.

To some degree, you have naturally responded to hope your entire life. During times of success, your enthusiasm automatically strengthened your relationship with hope. Your positive emotions naturally energized your hope. That said, when you are going through more difficult or discouraging times, you can still respond to hope in such a way that maintains your relationship with hope and increases your capacity to remain a hopeful person throughout your life.

You are in a symbiotic relationship with hope. As hope succeeds at getting you to try new things, you move forward in your life, thus fulfilling the purpose of hope!

Manifestations of Hope

Over the years, I have found that maintaining a healthy relationship with hope became easier once I grasped the concept that there are different manifestations of hope, each requiring their own types of responses. These manifestations include: *active hope*, *waning hope*, and *false hope.*

Active Hope

Active hope is the manifestation of hope we all know and love. It's the hope you feel. It's the stuff poets write about and singers sing about. *Active hope* sparks excitement in your heart and lets you believe that what you are seeking to do is surely possible and even likely. *Active hope* energizes you and generates that positive outlook you have at the beginning of your endeavors. You practically bubble over with enthusiasm when you bask in the warm, encouraging glow of *active hope.*

Responding to Active Hope

In order to keep active hope alive and engaged in your life, you should be willing to offer it at least one (if not all) of three responses: consideration, planning, and action.

> **Consideration** – The first response you should *always* be willing to offer your hope, whenever you find yourself becoming hopeful about anything, is *consideration*. Consideration can be as simple as pausing to think something

through, or as extensive as implementing a full-blown research and development project.

When you feel yourself becoming inspired by *active hope*, but then brush aside your hopeful idea without further consideration, you damage your relationship with hope. On the other hand, when you pause to at least consider an idea that hope has inspired in you, then you strengthen your relationship with hope because you've responded to it.

Planning – If, after considering a hopeful idea, you are still hopeful and would like to give your idea a fair chance at becoming a reality, then your next response to hope should be *planning*. Planning can be as simple as considering various ways to go about something, or as extensive as drafting a full-blown plan with tasks, a timeline, and a budget.

Planning is another way to respond to *active hope*. A good plan not only gives your hope a better chance at being realized, it infuses your hopeful ideas with enthusiastic energy.

Action – If you have carefully considered a hopeful idea, and have put together a viable plan for achieving it, then the only response left to offer your hope is *action*. While you are still in the rosy glow of *active hope*, there is no greater response you can offer your hopeful aspirations than that of action.

When you act on hope, you powerfully reinforce your capacity for future hope.

Waning Hope

When you are in the manifestation of *waning hope*, you don't feel particularly hopeful in the moment. It's the situation I referred to earlier when I wrote, *"you're not always going to feel it."* *Waning hope* comes on the heels of *active hope* and reflects the fact that some kind of discouragement, doubt, setback, or insecurity has reared its ugly head. *Waning hope* is that sinking feeling you get when things don't go the way you wanted or expected them to, and you begin to wonder if what you hoped for is even possible. Your thinking during times of *waning hope* will often run along the lines of: *I can't really do this. What's the point? I'm just wasting my time. What was I thinking?*

Responding to Waning Hope

Waning hope requires endurance, even as active hope falters.

> **Endurance** – When hope wanes, you must commit to *endurance* as you move through this stage of doubt. That is, you must be willing to continue on with your plans, at least until you can reevaluate your situation to learn what is really at the root of your *waning hope*.

Waning hope is a natural and predictable response to obstacles, mishaps, and insecurities that *always* show up sooner or later. It is during times of *waning hope* that you should review your personal history and approach. Past failures call for some reflection, and possibly a new approach, but they don't necessarily predict failure. You might need to push through some insecurities that are surfacing and getting the better of you. Or there may be a misunderstanding or lack of communication clouding the issue and causing things to seem bleaker than they actually are. You might even need to engage in some creative problem-solving. Perhaps your plans need tweaking. If, after some review (and possibly readjustment), your plans still seem viable, then carry on with them, even as your feelings vacillate between hope and hopelessness.

During times of waning hope, it helps to think of your plans like a navigational system. They are there for you to rely on when you can no longer find your way.

False Hope

And finally, there is the manifestation of *false hope. False hope* is inevitable. All of us will run up against it from time to time. *False hope* is hope that may have been fostered in misinformation or a miscalculation of some kind. You can try to mitigate your chances of experiencing *false hope* by carefully considering and planning things out well during the *active hope* phase. Still, changing circumstances or hidden factors can come to light well after you've begun to act on hope, and you can then find yourself in the grim reality that is *false hope*.

False hope is a devastating thing to experience. It can shatter your confidence and harm your capacity to hope in the future.

Responding to False Hope

In order to keep hope alive and capable of inspiring you throughout your life, your response to false hope should always be to "return to the drawing board."

Return to the Drawing Board – When you reach a point where you realize you've acted upon something that just doesn't have a chance of succeeding, then you need to *return to the drawing board* to reconsider your idea. It's important to review your initial decisions to try to learn what went wrong. What do you know now that you didn't know then? Is the situation redeemable, and, if so, how? Do you want to try again, perhaps with a new approach, or would you rather just cut your losses and move on to something else? What did you learn? In retrospect, what were the red flags? How can you avoid a similar situation in the future?

You certainly don't want to wallow in your disappointment. But by taking some time to review your situation and answer questions like these, you can gain valuable understanding into cause and effect, which will serve you when you engage in future hopeful endeavors.

When you run up against false hope, sometimes throwing in the towel and licking your wounds is inevitable. But if you can at least "return to the drawing board" long enough to consider what went wrong, then you've continued to respond to hope.

At the Very Least...

Of course, you don't have to chase every little hopeful idea that pops into your head. If you did that, you would dart from one thing to another more often than a dragonfly on a summer's day! But you shouldn't just ignore hope either. If you can, at the very least, pause to consider your hopeful ideas, then you have continued to respond to hope.

To Wish Is Not to Hope

Star light, star bright,
First star I see tonight,
I wish I may, I wish I might,

56

Have this wish I wish tonight.
—Anonymous

Wishing is a fanciful thing. It sparks our imaginations and allows us to visualize a better reality for ourselves—if only for a moment. We drop our wishes into fountains and send them up to the stars because we believe (on some level) that the only way they will come true is if they are granted to us.

Hope, on the other hand, is more substantial than a wish.

While a wish tends to stop at the wishing well, hope continues with us. Hope encourages us to do things that move us beyond imaginary fancies.

If you simply wish for something, then you are not really counting on having that thing in your life. Sure, it would be nice to have it, but you are pretty much relying on someone somewhere to grant it to you. On the other hand, when you begin *considering* ways to obtain something, and when you *plan* and *act* to create something in your life, then you have real hope of achieving it.

A wish engaged and acted upon becomes hope, whereas hope unacted upon remains but a wish.

It's That Important

Every day, I see people with enormous potential fail to realize their potential because their relationship with hope is weak. I myself have wasted years (that's plural) not accomplishing what I might have because my hope was fickle to nonexistent at the time.

I'm so grateful that my natural propensity for hope and op-timism eventually came back to me and is now a part of my constitution. I'm grateful that I was fortunate enough to chance upon a radio sermon (all those years ago), which introduced me to the concept that I can feed my hope to keep it alive and strong in my life. I would never have been able to *start over* successfully in my own life, let alone accomplish so much of what I've been able to do, had I not been able to maintain a hopeful spirit.

My hope for you is that you always remain hopeful, and that your hope inspires you to go on to accomplish great things.

Martin Luther said of hope,

"Everything that is done in the world is done by hope."

I believe that's true. All life must dare to hope!

No living thing continues well on its journey without some degree of hope. The stories of our lives won't be what they could be if we fail to hope. Without hope, even our bodies fail to thrive. Hope is that important.

Section Two:
Fresh & New

Seasons
Discoveries
Resistance
Saboteurs

Seasons

Chapter Five

Just as seasons change and years turn, our present days, as beloved as they may be, will fall into the past. When this happens, we will experience loss—sometimes profoundly so. It is during times of loss that we are called on to draw inward for a time, so that we might pause and adjust to a new reality. Then life goes on, and we must go on with it. It is the natural order of things that we do so.

Fresh and New

I don't know about you, but just thinking about the words *fresh and new* causes my spirit to lift a little. When I think of those words, my mind conjures up images like those of a mountain valley, dotted with flowers pushing up through patches of melting snow. I can also envision a spacious new home, fresh and clean, promising a new future to whoever moves into it. I can also imagine a beautiful bride in a white gown, radiating with happiness as she walks down the aisle to take the hand of the man she loves. These are the kinds of things I imagine when I think of *fresh and new*. Images like these make me feel good inside. They make me want to inhale—deeply.

Letting Go

But the thing about *fresh and new* is that you must be willing to relinquish something else to let it in.

As enchanting as the mountain valley may be when it is completely blanketed with snow, its snowy landscape will have to melt away in order for the flower-laced meadow to appear. The brand-new home, with its fresh start, will forever remain a fantasy if its potential new occupants can't summon enough resolve to leave their cramped yet familiar abode. And the beautiful bride walking down the aisle on her wedding day will surely have to leave aspects of her single self behind.

S*tarting over* carries with it an expectation that something *fresh and new* is about to come into your life. When approached optimistically, fresh starts can be exciting as well as healthy. They can energize and lift your spirit like flowers budding by the growing warmth of spring. But you can't fully receive anything *fresh and new*, let alone sustain it, if you can't let go of what you need to let go of from your past first.

When the Universe calls on you to do something fresh and new with your life, you must be willing to surrender something else to make space for it.

Letting go of what is no longer working for you isn't always going to be easy, but it will be necessary.

Loss

Because *starting over* requires some form of letting go, you will likely experience a sense of loss, on and off, as you move through the process. So be prepared for that. It's not unusual to have moments of incertitude, melancholia, pain (both emotional and physical), and even regrets, especially at the beginning.

But *starting over* also means that you are poised and ready to embark on a new chapter in life. It means that (on some level) you are ready to heed a new calling and contribute something different to your world—something the world needs for you to contribute.

If you can answer that call, and if you can experience your sense of loss while still choosing to remain focused on some new goals and aspirations, then, given enough time, your life will pivot into a *fresh and new* direction. You will eventually get to the point where you will be proud of yourself for having had the courage to let go of what you needed to let go of, so that you could move forward in your life and go on to accomplish something that, on a deeper level, you really wanted to do.

Letting go of old ways, which are neither serving you nor contributing to your personal growth, may cause you to feel a sense of loss for a time; that's normal. But try to keep moving forward anyway. These are life-changing moments that call on you to live a more purposeful life.

Feeling Loss Doesn't Mean You Made a Mistake

When you are on your journey of *starting over*, and you suddenly feel overwhelmed with pangs of loss for your past, it doesn't mean that you have made a mistake. It simply means that you have experienced people, places, and events, which you have truly loved and are now missing. It means that the seasons of your life, with all their beautiful memories, have turned once again, and you are remembering them.

So, go ahead and pause if you need to. Feel your pain for a time. Indulge in your precious memories and give them their place of pride in your heart and mind. But try to set a time limit for doing so if you can. Remember to return, once again, to your present-day desires and reality.

Continue to live, create, and build your new life, even as beloved memories tug at your heart and beg you to look back for a time. Your past is best honored when it's a part of a continuously and fully lived life.

Grief

Not only does some form of loss often precipitate your *starting over* journey, but *starting over* always brings about some form of loss. That means, to a greater or lesser degree, some form of grief will accompany you on your journey.

Everything passes,
Trees, flowers, tall meadow grasses,
The sun shines brightly, then sets the day,
Everything passes away.
—Gail Jenkins

I wrote that sad snippet of a poem when I was a young girl and my cat, Dusty, died. But as juvenile as it may be on one hand, this simple fact remains: everything passes. It's a truth as simple as it is constant and profound.

When you live your life in such a way that you truly love and connect with others, then, sooner or later, you're going to experience grief, because all things change, and all things pass.

Regardless, you must continue to love and connect in your life. Your spirit really can bear the pain of grief that accompanies loving and connecting with others, because your spirit was made to love and connect with others. That's how it thrives. Try to remember that...

Love, once experienced, is eternal, and connection is how you fully experience your life.

Getting Over Grief

There's a lot of talk today about working through or getting over grief. But my experience with grief has been that you never really get through or over it, because you never quite leave what is grieved for behind.

Grief becomes foundational in your life because your love for what has passed is foundational.

You can, however, come to fully live your life again. You can build, create, and serve again, even with grief. You can come to love again. And actually, it's your willingness to do so that, given time, will soften the acutely painful edges of your grief.

As grief lays itself down and spreads itself out into the foundation of your being, you must get to the point where you are willing to live, love, and participate in life again, even with grief. It's the new life you are willing to live that eventually softens the edges of your grief. It is the new life you are willing to live that celebrates and honors those who are no longer with you.

If you are grieving right now, just know that, given time, you can come to experience a rich and fulfilling life again. Often more so because your grief makes you profoundly aware of the fleeting nature of all things. That means you can recognize and relish your present loves so much more.

Taking It with You

Over time, I've come to realize that one of the great secrets to being able to let go and move forward after a loss is to mostly let go, but not to entirely let go.

If everything you love becomes foundational to who you are, then it's perfectly acceptable that you continue honoring who and what you love for your entire life.

You can always take something of everyone and everything you have ever loved with you into your future days, without stopping the forward momentum of your life. In fact, it is by doing so that your past continues to live on with you in a healthy way. However, if you stop living your life because you are in a prolonged state of mourning, then what you are missing remains a dead and mourned thing. If you can continue to live, love, and expand in your life, even as you grieve, then what you love continues to live, love, and expand with you.

It's your continued living, loving, and remembering that continues to animate and breathe life into everyone and everything you have ever loved.

The Sedona House

When I bought my beautiful house in Sedona, Arizona, it was the first real house I had ever owned. Sure, I have owned and lived in a few apartment-style condos in my past. And at various points in time, I have lived in houses owned by my parents and my grandparents. But this was the first single-family, detached house, with its two-car garage and front and back yards, that was all mine!

I spent several weeks visiting the local art galleries and picking out just the right pieces to build my décor around. My yard was pretty much dirt and gravel when I moved in, so I enjoyed choosing the plants and designing my own landscaping. Then there was the unfinished fireplace in the great room. I picked out three different shades of sandstone to frame it in with. Once it was complete, it was stunning! That fireplace became the focal point of the room. There was no doubt about it, I loved my Sedona house! It was my dream home by all accounts. I thoroughly enjoyed all the little projects I engaged in to infuse it with my own style and energy.

That said, there were moments, especially in the early days of moving in and fixing it up, when I found myself thinking about my past a lot. Then I'd experience what I can only describe as waves of grief. You see, my father had died a year prior to me buying the house, and my mother a decade before that. I missed them both terribly. Moving into my first house was something I wanted to share with them. I wanted to call them on the phone daily and tell them about every little thing I was doing. But I couldn't do that, could I?

The grief I felt over not having my family with me anymore was overwhelming at times. I can remember a day when I found myself sitting on a stool in the middle of my living room for what must have been hours, surrounded by unopened boxes, just missing my parents. Where I really wanted to be at the time was sitting on a stool in my mother's kitchen, snapping green beans for her as she prepared dinner. I wanted to look over at my father sitting in his recliner, leafing through the evening paper. I wanted to walk to school again, and toboggan down Hannon Street in the snow again. I wanted my past back so much that, at one point, I actually choked on my own breath. I ached to step through some magical window in time and go back to earlier days—to happier days when my family was still in my life.

When I finally came out of my malaise and got back to the task of unpacking and setting up my house again, I found myself putting out some things that reminded me of what I was missing so much. I filled my grandmother's crystal vase with wildflowers from the field next door and placed it on the kitchen counter. My grandmother loved picking the wildflowers that grew along the road in front of her house. She particularly loved the Queen Anne's lace and black-eyed Susans. Because of that memory, even walking over to the field to pick flowers reminded me of her, and it was comforting. I unpacked my mother's crocheted quilt and neatly folded it over the foot of the bed in the guest room. That quilt made the room look so cozy and inviting. I found a framed photo of my dad standing by a lake in his Army uniform. I dusted it off and positioned it just right on a shelf over my writing desk. The more I did little things like these to honor my past, the better I started to feel about my future.

As the weeks ticked by, I continued to find little ways to honor my past. I planted a crepe myrtle at the corner of the house in honor of my grandmother, who absolutely *loved* her crepe myrtle. I planted a row of roses along the side of the driveway to remember my mother, who was always clipping and deadheading her roses on summer mornings before it got too hot. I installed utility shelves in my garage, and a worktable that ran along the length of the back wall, similar to what Dad had done in his garage.

Of course, it was still my house. I decorated it around my Sedona art in a style that neither my parents nor grandparents would have appreciated. But I also managed to blend some beloved elements from my past into my current surroundings. It felt good to do so. It was like the people and places from my past were still there with me (respectfully so, not overwhelmingly so), enhancing my new home and bringing their beautiful loving energy into my present days.

Whether it's loved ones in spirit, or a past career, or a house, or even a special moment in time, try to find ways to bring something from your beloved past into your present days. In this way, everyone and everything you have ever loved remains a living part of who you are today.

Nostalgia

Sometimes, when I'm feeling especially nostalgic, I'll drive by one of my old houses in one of my old neighborhoods. When I do, however, I never quite see what I loved so much about them anymore. Other people have moved in, and their style and energy have replaced what I remember. My beloved memories are more a part of who I am today, than they are any one structure or place associated with my past.

And that is as it should be, because our past can't continue to live in the past. The past is gone. But the past can continue to live on through us as we continue to embrace our lives.

Love is a powerful thing. Love is a living thing. True love isn't attached to any one thing or moment in your past. True love lives in you. By fully living your life today, you continue to honor the loves from your past and allow them to continue expressing themselves through you.

The Void

There is a phenomenon that occurs in our human experience that I've come to refer to as *the void*. Entering *the void* often comes on the heels of loss or grief. But it can also occur whenever there is a major change in life, or about to be.

The void is kind of hard to explain, exactly. But I'm going to give it my best shot, because understanding *the void* and what it feels like, as well as what it is calling on us to do, is an essential part of being able to move forward in life.

When you find yourself in the void, you find yourself immersed in a feeling of detachment. There's an emptiness to the void—a stillness. The void is definitely a place where you exist alone for a time. Other people may be around you, physically, and you may go through the motions of everyday life, but you will feel somewhat isolated and detached, nonetheless.

Some people believe *the void* is a type of loneliness. When it comes down upon them, they seek to fill it with as many distractions as they can in order to shake it off. Others interpret it as a kind of depression. That's easy enough to understand since it often comes on the heels of loss, so sadness and grief can accompany it. When you first start to experience *the void*, you may find it difficult to imagine a positive future for yourself. So, in that sense, *the void* can trigger anxieties and fears about the future.

But as awful as all of that seems, I believe that *the void* actually serves a positive purpose in our lives and, therefore, it represents a sacred time.

The purpose of the void is to bring you to a pause, so that you can consider and adjust to a life change. The void calls on you to do a life review of sorts, so that you can make important decisions about your life going forward.

When life brings you into *the void*, it brings you into a Zen-like consciousness. You are alone with the Universe, and the Universe feels like a vast and empty place. That's because the Universe is vast with potential, but the potential is unrealized. Therefore, the Universe feels vastly empty.

You feel isolated in the void because your path forward is something only you can choose. You feel a bit outside of time and space in the void because what "has been" is slipping away, and what "will be" has yet to be established.

The Starship Enterprise

One of the best metaphors I can think of to help further explain what *the void* is like, would be that of the *Starship Enterprise* traveling through space. As she journeys, stars and other heavenly bodies slip by her windows like streaks of light. Then, typically, something in the story changes, prompting the *Enterprise* to slow down and eventually come to a stop. Celestial bodies come into focus and seem to hang in space with the starship. Everything is paused. Everything is still. Eventually, the captain considers some new information, makes some new decisions, and issues a new directive. That's usually when the *Enterprise* slowly pivots before launching off in a new direction—her new mission is engaged!

That pause, when the *Enterprise* just kind of hangs there and idles in space, is very much like *the void*.

The void is a pause in life on the cusp of change. Just the fact that you are in it means that change is beckoning. It means that you are being given a say in your future's direction. That's a powerful moment! That's a sacred moment.

My Personal Experience with the Void

My life has undergone so many transitions that I've become fairly accustomed with *the void* and what it feels like. I no longer fear *the void* or seek to escape it. I've learned to pause with *the void* and acknowledge that I'm in a profound and pivotal moment. I try to imagine that *the void* is a safe place where I can rest in the arms of the Universe for a time. I know that life is about to change. I know that I'm being given permission to pause and reflect for a time. The very presence of *the void* tells me this. I also know that if I'm brave enough to stand in my own power and make some important decisions, then I'll be able to co-create my future in some positive way. That's the real purpose of *the void*. That's what *the void* is all about.

On the other hand…

If I fail to take advantage of the self-reflection that *the void* is calling on me to do, and if I fail to make the important decisions and changes that I'm being given an opportunity to make, then it's been my experience that *the void* comes down upon me over and over again until its emptiness really does become a depression. In addition, if I manage to just shake off *the void* and fill its emptiness with distractions until it passes, then my life remains in status quo until events occur that shape my future for me, regardless of how I feel about them. Either way, I fail to exercise my personal power in life. And either way, I fail to identify and seize upon some blessed gifts and opportunities that were once there for me.

The Gift

Life is a gift. We are all so privileged to be here on this planet, contributing to its story with our own. And, just like our living Earth, your life will have its seasons. You will have your seasons of hope and new beginnings; you will have your seasons of love and laughter; you will have your seasons of loss and letting go; and you will have your seasons of rest and recovery from the various storms and ill winds that blow through your life. Every one of your seasons is part of the cycle of life.

"Under every grief and pine, runs a joy with silken twine."
—William Blake

When joy and love come into your life, they come with loss in tow. Go ahead and enjoy and love anyway. Because it will be all the seasons in your life, collectively, that weave themselves into the tapestry of your life, making it a rich, intricate, and profoundly beautiful thing. Dare to live such a beautiful life.

As long as your seasons continue to turn, you have the gift of life. As long as you have the gift of life, you have a chance to live your life with more authenticity and purpose. Therefore, do your best to enjoy and weather all your seasons. Dare to fully live your life, knowing that the Universe is always going to be there for you, helping you along the way, once you invite it in and make it your intention that it does so.

Discoveries

Chapter Five

"Not until we are lost do we begin to understand ourselves."
—Henry David Thoreau

When sudden life changes occur, it doesn't matter so much why they occur; or how young or old you are at the time; or how prepared or unprepared you think you are; shifting circumstances will push you into a new world with new rules, regardless of how you feel about it. That said, when approached with the right mindset, these changes can be very positive. They are almost always tied to some higher purpose. Although all change comes with challenges, and some of those challenges can be straight-up traumatic, change also bears a gift.

Once approached with the right mindset, change is almost always tied to some higher calling, which, on some level, your spirit wants you to engage in.

Once you can accept and rise to the challenge of change, you will often be faced with two choices: 1) Adjust to a new way of functioning where you are, or 2) Take your life in an entirely different direction. Both choices will bring about their own unique challenges, gifts, and lessons, and both will contribute to your personal growth in some way. Whichever way you choose, just know that you will be learning and experiencing new things and evolving as a soul at an existential level.

New environments beg you to shed self-imposed restrictions and old aspects of yourself that may not be serving you anymore.

A Period of Discovery

When you are *starting over* in life, because of the monumental changes happening to you, it's not unusual to go through periods of feeling lost or disconnected. You might even find yourself struggling with your sense of identity as you navigate ways that are unfamiliar to you. Feeling a bit clumsy or out of place at times is predictable. In fact, I'm predicting it now. So, do yourself a favor and cut yourself some slack. Try not to obsess too much over how well you are or are not progressing, especially in the beginning. Instead, try going with the flow of things for a while and mostly observe. There is a learning curve to *starting over*. Also, try not to get overly caught up in your emotions as they vacillate between optimism and discouragement. Understand that you have entered a very predictable and natural *period of discovery.*

You're not expected to have everything figured out from the get-go, but you are expected to keep moving forward in your life and experiment a little as you find your new way in a new world.

Try not to beat yourself up too much if you find yourself changing venues more often than you typically would. You're not being wishy-washy here (well, yes, you are, but this time it's okay). You're being experimental!

Experimentation is a tool that's going to help you discover who you are in today's reality, as well as what you want to be doing in the next chapter of your life.

Second Chances

Starting over can be fraught with anxiety. I'm not going to pretend otherwise. But it can also be an exciting time! That's because it offers you a second chance to do more of what is truly right and meaningful for you. It offers you a chance to make different choices and establish a better fit this time around. That's an incredible opportunity that not everyone gets to realize. Some folks are bound to earlier choices that stopped working for them years ago. Others go into their later years with some serious regrets—regrets they could have rectified at various points in time, but didn't, because they didn't have the opportunity or courage to do so.

You've changed. The world has changed. It only makes sense that some of your choices will change as well.

So, grant yourself permission to go through some trial and error. That way, when you are ready to start committing to things again, you'll have a better understanding of what you need in today's reality to feel complete.

You don't want to just reestablish yourself so that you're up and functioning. You want to reestablish yourself in ways that bring more fulfillment and purpose into your life. Now is not the time to push back on those things you've always wanted to do, because…

When you come to the end of your life's journey, unrealized potential isn't going to matter as much as what you've actually done and experienced.

Transitional times are these golden opportunities to identify and explore those things you've always wanted to do. *Starting over* clears space so that you might add more richness and purpose to your life.

Looking Under Rocks

Looking under rocks is a phrase I like to use when I'm experimenting with different scenarios—that is, when I'm trying them on for size. You too will *look under rocks* as you try out new things. You will *look under rocks* when you explore different career paths, academic avenues, hobbies, talents, interests, relationships, geographical areas to live, or even when you try out different forms of self-expression or personal style.

> *Looking under rocks can help you identify what you want to do next and clarify the legacy you want to leave behind.*

My Year of Jobs

When I first moved to Sedona, I had to find a place to live, obviously, but I also had to find a source of income. After all, I wasn't independently wealthy! I wanted something that paid the bills, but I also wanted to do something that I really loved doing. Let's face it, I didn't make a 2,400-mile trip across the country to simply exist. I had been existing just fine in Maryland. I moved away from my home state so that I could exercise more personal freedom and independence, and hopefully establish myself as a successful woman on my own terms. I needed to know that I was capable of that kind of success. I also wanted the flexibility to experiment a little, without worrying about the prying eyes or judgements of others who were accustomed to having an influence over my life. I also love hiking (it's a passion, really), so I wanted to make sure that in whatever I did for income, I still had the time and proximity to be able to hike in the beautiful red rocks and high-desert wilderness that surround the town.

It was a nice dream to start off with. And honestly, looking back from a future perspective, I can see that I've been able to accomplish all of it. That said, building my "happily ever after" life in the Great American Southwest turned out to be a little harder than I thought it was going to be. "Happily ever after" didn't just drop into my lap (and really, it rarely does). In fact, I had to engage in an extensive *period of discovery* as I found my way in a completely different world than what I was used to. I had to get comfortable with the fact that it really was okay to walk away from certain situations that weren't good fits for me.

Case in point: when I first moved to Sedona, I had five different jobs in one year! It was just crazy! It got to the point where I didn't want to call my friends and family back east anymore, because I didn't want to have to explain to them why (yet again) I was working for a different employer! Honestly, it was becoming embarrassing!

You see, Sedona is a tourist town, which means it's transient by nature. This transiency extends to its workforce. Also, many of the employers there are small mom-and-pop businesses that experience cash flow problems several times a year. Add those two conditions together and you've got frustration on both sides of the coin. Poor pay and impossible performance expectations cause frustration and resentment in employees, prompting many to quit after a season or two, which in turn fuels frustration and resentment in their employers. It's a catch-22 dynamic, and the job market in Sedona is entrenched in it.

What I didn't understand when I first moved there was that halfway-decent jobs were few and far between. Folks who were fortunate enough to have them often went through a string of disappointing work experiences before they finally landed in a good fit for them.

Below, I've shared a brief accounting of my five Sedona jobs, because I think these misadventures, as well as the naiveté I started them out with, are good examples of why it's so important to *look under rocks* and give yourself the freedom to go through a *period of discovery*.

Job #1

My first Sedona job was at a gift shop that paid minimum wage. I thought it would be a fun little job that would help pay the bills until I figured out what the heck I wanted to be doing with the rest of my life. That assessment changed, however, once I started working there. To make a long story short, I don't think the store manager liked me very much. No matter what I did, or how hard I tried to follow her instructions, she was constantly criticizing me, usually in front of customers. It was demoralizing, to say the least. It got to the point where I couldn't do anything right. Add to that the fact that my paychecks were unreliable (they often bounced on my first attempts to deposit them), and I think you can understand why, after only two months of working there, I gave up on this job and gave notice.

Job #2

My next job was a big improvement, or so it seemed. It was at an upscale jewelry store in uptown Sedona. I started out making five dollars more an hour right off the bat! I got along super well with the store's manager, as well as the owner. That said, it wasn't long before another troubling dynamic began to rear its ugly head. Just before I was hired, most of the store's long-standing employees had been fired. This caused the remaining employees to become extremely competitive, to the point that (in my opinion) they were becoming overly aggressive and even manipulative. It soon became apparent that I only had two choices: either play that game and play it better than anyone else, or get the heck out of Dodge while my reputation and dignity were still intact. Since I didn't move to Sedona to get drawn into that kind energy, once again, I gave notice and found another job—a third job.

Job #3

My third job was a lucky break! Without any prior experience, I landed a position at one of Sedona's most renowned art galleries. It was located in Tlaquepaque, a Spanish-style arts and crafts village modeled after the real village of Tlaquepaque, Mexico (now part of Guadalajara).

Tlaquepaque in Sedona is incredibly beautiful and romantic. It has Mexican-tiled accents throughout, along with fountains, archways, string lights, shops, and restaurants, all lining cobblestone streets. Its landscaping incorporates these ginormous old sycamore trees, as well as numerous gardened nooks and courtyards. At the center of it all is a mission-style church with a bell tower that chimes out every hour. The setting alone was enough to make this job delightful.

I was very happy to be working there for the first few months. I admired the artist and enjoyed sharing his creative visions. My happiness at work was reflected in my sales, which were good from the start and kept getting better. That is, until Sedona's temperate spring gave way to summer's stifling heat, and foot traffic and art sales dropped off dramatically. That's when my sales dropped off as well, and the artist began acting peculiar. He began spying on me by lurking behind plants and hiding in the closet (presumably to critique my sales technique). This made me increasingly nervous and, consequently, my sales got even worse. One morning, I pulled back the curtain covering the utility room and screamed because there he was, standing in the dark. I screamed! He screamed! He admonished me for scaring him! I responded to him in kind because he had scared me first! It was all pretty awful, and we both ended up having a bad morning. Things only got worse between us in the following days. We were constantly bickering and misinterpreting each other's intentions. It got to the point where I hated getting up and going to work in the morning. And so, once again (ay, yi yi!), I gave notice and found job number four!

Job #4

This job was always going to be a temporary gig. I had no delusions of grandeur there. I only took it to get away from job number three.

Job number four was at a little jewelry store (also in Tlaquepaque) that was rumored to be going through some financial difficulties. It turned out to be an okay job, really. I was grateful to get it at the time. The rumor about financial hardship, however, turned out to be true enough because, eventually, the owner of the business packed up all his wares in the middle of the night and skipped out on his rent. He posted a sign on the front door, which read, *Will be back shortly,* and someone scribbled over it, *Not bloody likely!* (Ah, the drama in Tlaquepaque! But I digress…) None of this really affected me too much because, even while I was working there, I was actively seeking other employment. I always held onto the belief that, sooner or later, something just right would come along. And sure enough, it did!

Job #5

My fifth job was at another art gallery. I loved everything about this place! I loved its beautiful setting (again, in Tlaquepaque). I loved the owners. They were always good to me and did little things to show their staff just how much they appreciated us. I loved the artists who showcased there. I loved the customers who loved the gallery as much as I did. Before long, I was selling at the top of my game again and I stayed there, even during the slow seasons! And, because I was being paid a decent wage and commission this time, I ended up making more money than I ever could have made at any of my other past Sedona jobs! I really loved this job, and I was good at it. I hit the jackpot this time, and I knew it!

It may have taken some time, and some trial and error, and it certainly took some persistent hope and faith in my future, but once my employment situation synergized with my personality, skillset, and needs, I thrived! Subsequently, the gallery thrived as well!

There's no shame in taking missteps when you are seeking to reestablish yourself, but there is a directive: take the time you need to discover where your talents lie and what gives you a greater sense of fulfillment, then put your energy there.

Looking back, I'm glad I gave myself permission to *look under rocks* and experiment with different workplace scenarios. I'm glad I followed my instincts and didn't settle at any one place that wasn't a good fit for me. As it was, I continued to move into better and better scenarios until I landed somewhere that was just right for me—kind of like Goldilocks!

Harmonizing What You Do with Who You Are

I don't think anyone reading this right now wants to just get by in their life. Where's the joy in that?

As things stand, you've got years of experiences, observations, and wisdom you could be tapping into and bringing to the table. Trust me when I say that you've already got skills you could be applying towards building a more gratifying life for yourself. But you don't have an infinite amount of time to do it. Therefore, it's going to be paramount that you can identify and hone in on things that are right for you, so you can start living your better life sooner rather than later.

Not only do you deserve to be in situations that fit you better, energetically, but it's the only way you're going to thrive.

Experimentation is a tool that will help you discover what components you need to have in place to rebuild your life your way. But in order to use that tool efficiently, you're going to have to develop a particular skill as well. You're going to have to have a skill for *harmonizing what you do with who you are.*

"Harmonizing what you do with who you are" is a cornerstone in successful living. It invites more synergy into your life, which enables you to live your most productive life.

Sensitivity and Grace

Harmonizing what you do with who you are has two components to it. First, you need the *sensitivity* to recognize what's right for you (and what's not), and second, you need the *grace* (or flow) to align your life accordingly.

Sensitivity

Did you know you were born with a sensitivity that is always seeking to alert you to what fits with your energy and what doesn't?

You have, as part of your innate human nature, an inner sensitivity that is always seeking to communicate important information to you. This sensitivity speaks to you through your feelings. So, regardless of what you have come to believe about your feelings up until now, it's crucial that you don't discount them or shut them down in any way.

You can always determine whether or not it's appropriate to express your feelings, or to act on them in the given moment, because sometimes it won't be. And, you can always examine your feelings to determine if they are indeed rooted in the reality of things, because sometimes they won't be! But whatever you do, don't ignore your feelings—not now. Try to open yourself up to them instead. Observe them. At the very least, acknowledge your true feelings in private if you must, because…

It's going to be through your feelings of right or wrong (in any given situation) that you will come to discover the right paths for you.

When Sensitivity Speaks

Your sensitivity to what's going on around you and how it's affecting you is something that's always available to you, and it's always seeking to communicate with you. Your sensitivity communicates with you through your feelings, and your feelings in turn communicate in two ways: through your *emotions*, and through your *body*.

You already know your emotions reflect your feelings, but did you know your body reflects your feelings as well? Your body has something important to say about the situations you are in and how well they resonate with you, energetically.

When you are seeking to tap into your sensitivity about something, don't forget to listen to your body as well. Both your emotional and physical sense of well-being are going to be indicators of what's right or wrong for you at this particular stage in your life.

Think of your sensitivity as a compass and your feelings as its points. Together, they guide you this way and that until you arrive at your best fit.

When you live a life that fits you better, you feel better and accomplish more. When you feel better and accomplish more, you're able to live a more gratifying and expressive life. Who doesn't want that?

Oversensitivity

Have you ever been accused of being oversensitive? Chances are, whoever said this to you triggered your feelings of being disrespected, misinterpreted, violated, discounted, insulted, mocked, or otherwise offended, and you responded according-ly. Every time you've been accused of being oversensitive, one of two things was probably happening: either you were right in your assessment of the situation, and you needed to stand up for yourself (in which case, kudos to you for speaking up!); or you misjudged the situation and overreacted. When you over-react (or wrongly react), then the real issue isn't your sensitivity, it's your misinterpretation of and subsequent reaction to what you are sensing.

When you overreact, your sensitivity isn't the problem. Your reaction is the problem. Although it's often appropriate to temper your reactions and explore the truth of a situation before issuing a knee-jerk response, you should never seek to stifle your sensitivity.

And the reason for that is this:

Your sensitivity is an indicator of what's going on around you and how it's affecting you. You will absolutely need that input if you're going to build the most fulfilling life for yourself.

The Motion Detector Light

A good example of how your sensitivity works, and how you should be responding to it at any given moment, would be that of a backyard motion detector light. Let's say that the light goes on a few times during the night, waking you up. You're probably not going to jump up out of bed and run down the stairs, only to burst out into your backyard with your shotgun in hand, each and every time the light goes on. Right? And you're probably not going to disconnect the motion detector light either, because it's there for a reason. What you are most likely going to do is lie there for a moment (maybe you'll get up to look out the window), and then you'll make a judgement call as to whether there's really something going on that needs your attention or not. Quite often there's not. Your sensitivity works the same way.

You may need to develop better interpretational and reactive skills when it comes to managing your feelings, but you shouldn't seek to disconnect from them.

As you go about discovering your *fresh and new* world, and as you *look under rocks* and explore new things, try to stay tapped into your sensitivity throughout. You'll want to be both analytical and sensitive as you work your way through all the new situations you are encountering.

Your sensitivity is a gift that, once understood and managed well, will serve you your entire life.

Grace

The second way to go about *harmonizing what you do with who you are* is by developing *grace* in your life.

Grace, as I'm referring to it here, is a fluidity in life—it's a flow. You achieve a graceful life when you make choices that better align with who you are.

If sensitivity allows you to recognize what you need in order to lead a more harmonious life, then grace is the act of harmonizing.

You move into a more graceful life when you make more personally authentic choices.

Those choices might include changes in diet, activities, clothing, style, sleep patterns, schedules, relationships, jobs, careers, locations, houses, friends, majors, habits, beliefs, medications, doctors, advisors, … and the list goes on.

Of course, there will always be those things you won't be able to change, or won't want to for one reason or another, and that's okay. Life is always going to be a little messy, and the idea that everything must be in perfect order at all times is pretty much delusional thinking. Perfection is just not possible in a living world with living beings, each making their own life choices. That said…

Even small changes, where and when you can make them, can have a profoundly positive effect on your life. They are still tangible steps in better "harmonizing what you do with who you are."

Old Mindsets

For some of us, honoring our sensitivities and experimenting with our lives (especially later in life) are counterintuitive. That's because we were raised to reject such notions in favor of pragmatism. We were taught that there are certain ways respectable people live and behave, and to do otherwise is equivalent to failure. A common way of thinking, which is rooted in days gone by, is that good people living good lives are primarily focused and stable. They don't dither-dather. They certainly don't allow their sensitivities to get the better of them.

Men, in particular, were taught to toughen up and remain emotionally detached. They were taught to do whatever they had to do to remain committed to their original choices. Anything less than that was seen as a weakness.

Women, on the other hand, were expected to be more emotional by nature. That said, they were also expected to stifle emotions that were viewed as unbecoming, such as discontentment, opposition, and anger. Women were also expected to defer on their individual desires in favor of the more traditional roles assigned to them.

Anyone seeking to create a better life for him or herself— one that was authentic, expressive, and personally fulfilling— was likely to be judged as foolish, selfish, and (if a woman) unattractive.

Genuine Strength

Let me just say that committing to power through a certain amount of discontent in order to accomplish an important goal in life really does make you a stronger, more capable person. I'm not going to discount that. But you're not meant to live your entire life in a state of discontent. You're just not. Especially not as you age! That kind of resolve doesn't equate to strength anymore. In fact, it can be demoralizing and deplete your energy, opening the doors for illness and depression. It can leave you with some serious regrets later on in life.

When your concept of strength no longer serves you, when it wears you down and chips away at your constitution instead, then it's failing you. That's when your sensitivity needs to be engaged—big time! That's when you need to look for ways to realign your life with more authenticity and grace.

Experimenting with your life (by *looking under rocks* and going through a *period of discovery*) so that you can make better decisions for yourself, doesn't reflect weakness; it reflects strength. It enables you to make choices that better *harmonize what you do with who you are*, which results in you becoming a stronger, more capable person. You no longer have the energy drain that an ill-fitting life generates. As a result, your confidence grows. You find that you have more passion and energy available to you as you face future challenges, and hopefully go on to serve your world in some better way. That's genuine strength!

A New Day Dawns

When you are *starting over*, it doesn't matter whether you are nineteen or ninety. You are still like a fawn in the forest, venturing out from your safe and familiar thicket for the first time. A new day dawns! The land stretching out before you is mysterious, vast, and daunting at first. But if your instincts are intact, you will still be drawn forward and will eventually figure out how to function in your *fresh and new* world.

Make no mistake, your sensitivity is instinctive and aligned with the natural order of things. It is an instrument of guidance in your life.

So, give yourself permission to feel your way as you explore new territory. Learn the lay of the land. Try out new things. Stay connected to your instincts. All of these things will serve you as you are figuring out what to do next.

That said, don't forget to also have some fun. It's imperative to take the time to simply enjoy your life.

Your joy will fuel your vital life force and become a part of who you are as a soul—if you allow it to.

"Seize the wonder and the uniqueness of today.
Recognize that throughout this beautiful day, you have an incredible number of opportunities to move your life into the direction you want to go."
—Steve Maraboli

91

Resistance

Chapter Six

Have you ever had days of feeling like you were stuck, energetically? Or maybe you've had weeks, or months, or dare I say years of feeling like you were stuck in a rut? You're not accomplishing what you've set out to do, but you can't seem to snap out of it either. It's not that you don't have greater aspirations. You do! You know you should be accomplishing more in your life. You know you should be utilizing your time better. Yet there you are, energetically stuck.

This feeling of being stuck, this immobilization, is a type of resistance, and we all experience it from time to time.

Resistance can be triggered by many things for many reasons. But the resistance I want to focus on here is your resistance to change, and that can include your resistance to fully engaging in life once change needs to occur.

The part of you that is resisting is the part that fears letting go. Life may not have been perfect the way it was, but at least you understood who you were and how things worked.

We often resist losing the familiarity of our past, even as our past is slipping away.

Starting Over Triggers Resistance (a personal story)

A few years ago, I entered the first phase of what would develop into a major life crisis. It was a one-two-three knockout series of events that involved health, finances, and eventually my sense of self-worth.

The first phase of this collective crisis concerned health. I came down with a mystery illness that took the medical community years to sort out to the point where I could fully function again. By the time all the right labs, diagnoses, and causes and effects were untangled and understood, the event had taken its toll on my body and life. As I've already referred to in earlier chapters, it turned out I had developed a chronic thyroid disorder, probably triggered by a lupus flare-up, possibly triggered by a viral event. Talk about the domino effect! It was exactly this cascading series of events that made a diagnosis so difficult to reach and eventually treat.

Although some of my symptoms improved with medication, I continued to have these weird muscular and neurological issues. I lost overall agility and strength. I couldn't sweat properly anymore. I had tingling sensations in my lower arms and feet. But the most debilitating effects by far showed up in my muscles. My muscles would either be weak and floppy, or involuntarily flexed and rigid. This was a painful condition that sometimes lasted for months on end. Imagine trying to sleep with your muscles permanently flexed. It's pretty much impossible. So, add insomnia to the mix. I was prescribed muscle relaxers and nerve blockers to address some of the issues, and they worked to a degree, but then I felt like I couldn't think clearly during the day. I also noticed that I was experiencing more muscle and tendon injuries while on those medications.

I was deep into a complicated and life-altering health crisis, which predictably led to a life-altering financial crisis, and then to a full-blown identity crisis.

In those early days of feeling sick, I knew that I could relieve some of my physical, mental, and financial hardships if only I sold my Sedona house. It was a no-brainer, really. Because if I did that, then I would be able move into a smaller, more manageable house. I would be able to pay down my exploding medical debt. And, perhaps most importantly, I would be able to take the downtime I needed to figure out what the heck was going on with my body and give myself a halfway decent chance at recovering.

It was a great plan, alright. I was lucky to be in a position to do it! The problem was, I wasn't doing it. You see, I didn't want to let go of my beloved Sedona house. It was my dream house by all accounts! I didn't want to have to move either. I loved my neighborhood and my neighbors. With all my being, I just wanted life to go back to the way it had been before I got sick. Anything less than that seemed unfathomable.

I refused to acknowledge the fact that my life had changed beyond anything I could control or reconcile anymore. But my life had changed, and it was calling on me to change with it. Still, I resisted that call. I carried on as I was, where I was (coping, striving, and declining), for as long as I could possibly manage it. There was no doubt about it, I was in the full throes of some powerful resistance.

As a result, my muscular and neurological issues didn't get better. If anything, they got worse. Maintenance issues began piling up around the house, to the point where everything was looking embarrassingly shabby. I wasn't performing well at work either (when I was there, that was). My performance and attendance slipped so much, it's amazing I didn't get fired (or maybe that was coming down the pike). And, because I kept cutting back on my hours at work, my finances slipped into an abysmal state. Looking back, my resistance to inevitable change didn't serve me, it only prolonged my suffering. My resistance made life much harder than it had to be.

Starting over is a call to change, and, even in the best of circumstances, that call can trigger resistance.

In an act of sheer survival, I was finally able to put my house on the market. That's when I *started over* again in my life. That's also when my life started to shift into a better trajectory, and the many damaged areas of my life began to finally recover.

After selling my house, I found a lovely, less expensive, light-filled home in the Verde Valley, just south of Sedona. I found myself, once again, in a great neighborhood with great neighbors. But perhaps most importantly, I had resources again, both in time and money. That gave me the means to consult with various health specialists and experiment with different techniques and therapies to help with my physical recovery.

You see, waiting for me on the other side of my resistance was a better life. I can honestly say that I have never felt as competent, or as self-assured, or as satisfied in life as I have since letting go of the Sedona house. In fact, if I could go back in time and do things differently, I would have sold the house much sooner than I did. I know now that I wasted far too much time struggling to hold onto a house, almost exclusively to my detriment.

Mine is a common testimonial, really. I hear different versions of this same story from other people sharing their own *starting over* experiences with me. I think one of the reasons why so many of us are happier once we do finally muster up the courage to let go of whatever it is we're clinging so tightly to, is because...

We are most satisfied when our spirits are satiated, and, more often than not, it's at a spiritual level that we are being called to change.

That's a pretty bold statement when you stop to think about it, because it suggests that unfortunate circumstances, which bring about major life changes, are somehow tied to a higher calling. And truth be told, that's exactly what I believe now.

Regardless of the circumstances that bring you to it, starting over is always an opportunity to create a more authentic and purposeful life for yourself, especially when you make it your intention to do so.

You are meant to be living an authentic and purposeful life! The part of you that is resisting change isn't allowing you to do that.

What Is Resistance?

Resistance, as it relates to starting over, is a disinclination to act when you should be moving your life forward in some way.

It's usually triggered by a need to move beyond your familiarities and comfort zone. Sometimes, the need to move on can be so disconcerting, so overwhelming, that a part of you would rather just shut down and not have to deal with it. And sometimes, that's exactly what you do! You shut down, to the point where you aren't accomplishing much of anything anymore.

All of this might make resistance seem like a big, bad thing, but at its core, it's not. Most resistance, once met and worked through, turns out to be good for you. Regardless of how you respond to it initially, good resistance isn't calling on you to shut down; it's calling on you to build up and work through it.

Good resistance isn't there to stop you. It's there to strengthen you as you move through it and forward with your life.

Types of Resistance

When you find yourself becoming stuck in the energetic muck that is your resistance, then, based on my experience, either one of three things is most likely happening to you: 1) Your resistance is presenting you with a good, healthy challenge; or 2) It's alerting you to the fact that something important needs to be revisited; or 3) It's disabling your progress in life. Therefore, there are actually three types of resistance that are worth discussing and understanding better: *challenging resistance*, *intuitive resistance*, and *debilitating resistance*.

Once you can recognize the type of resistance you're up against, then you'll have a better chance at managing it. Once you can effectively manage your resistance, then you can effectively push through it and get on with the business of fully living your life again!

Challenging Resistance

Challenging resistance is just what its name implies: it's resistance that challenges you. It insists that you try just a little harder than your current comfort level to achieve an important goal in life. *Challenging resistance* is actually a good type of resistance because, once met and worked through, it strengthens your constitution.

By taking on challenging resistance and pushing through it, you not only go on to achieve important goals in life, but aspects of your character improve. Your ability to focus sharpens. Your resolve for setting and achieving future goals strengthens.

The Mountain

A good example of *challenging resistance* would be that of climbing a mountain. The first thing you will need to do to climb a mountain is to set your goal to climb a mountain. Then you might want to prepare for mountain climbing. You might want to stock your backpack with important mountain climbing supplies, such as a fully charged cell phone, water, food, rain gear, sunscreen, and whatever else you think you might need during your climb. Then you set out to climb your mountain.

On the way up, you'll push through your resistance to rock, brush, weather, gravity, fatigue, breathlessness, and whatever else comes your way, until you finally come to stand on the mountain's summit and gaze out over the sweeping vista below. As you stand there, on the pinnacle of your success, something in you changes. Something fortifies. You are not quite the same person coming down off the mountain as you were going up. That's because your constitution has strengthened as you pushed through your resistance and succeeded in reaching your goal.

Pushing through challenging resistance not only takes you to the top of your proverbial mountain and changes your perspective of the world, but you then get to carry that accomplishment and expanded view with you wherever you go.

Intuitive Resistance

Intuitive resistance is another type of good resistance. I believe it's actually a form of communication from your psyche, trying to get your attention. Think of it as an extension of your instincts. When *intuitive resistance* kicks in, it prompts you to hesitate because it has an important message for you.

Maybe you're on the edge of getting sick, or exhausted, or burnt out, and you really do need to slow down a bit. Or maybe you're on the wrong path in life. Or maybe there's a better way to go about doing something. Or maybe, deep down, you're not really sure you want what you thought you wanted. These are the kinds of situations that might trigger your *intuitive resistance,* which in turn begs you to pause and not act so fast.

To identify whether your resistance might be intuitive or not, try asking yourself some enlightening questions:

- Am I going about things in the right way?
- What's on the other side of this resistance?
- What are the probable benefits and consequences of nonaction?
- What are the probable benefits and consequences of taking action?
- What are my real goals here?
- Is this what I really want, deep down, or is something else calling to me?
- Am I unprepared?

- Does the situation at hand resonate with my highest good?
- Am I or anyone else going to be harmed by my actions?
- Am I getting sick?
- Am I overextending myself?

Questions like these can help you identify whether or not you are dealing with some type of *intuitive resistance*. If you suspect that you are, then pause for a moment, take the pressure off yourself to act, and think things through a bit more.

Intuitive resistance is slowing you down for a reason. It's trying to bring something important to your attention. Intuitive resistance is another type of good resistance because it's communication from your higher self. It's asking you to look into a situation more thoroughly.

Once you've given the situation at hand a little more thought and consideration, and once your decisions (whichever way they fall) sit better with you, then I think you'll find that your resistance is easing. If you choose to move forward again with your plans, you'll feel much better doing so.

Debilitating Resistance

If, however, your resistance isn't building up your character and strength; and if it isn't alerting you to a better way of going about something; and if it's just some undefinable lethargy that's got you stuck in a rut that's not really serving you anymore; then there is every chance that something else is going on beneath the surface. There may be some latent fear, doubt, or belief system, which is rearing its ugly head and fueling your resistance. This type of resistance doesn't serve you; it debilitates you. Therefore, I'm referring to it as *debilitating resistance*.

Debilitating resistance is a common and particularly tenacious type of resistance that immobilizes you. It often seems irrational. The key to managing it is to first recognize it for what it is, and then to take steps to weaken its hold over you. Once you can do that, then you can push through it, just as you would with any other type of good resistance.

Each and every one of us will run up against *debilitating resistance* at one time or another. When we do, it can be an obstinate little bugger! *Debilitating resistance* doesn't strengthen you; it does just the opposite. It keeps you from moving forward and realizing important milestones in your life. *Debilitating resistance* is typically subconsciously triggered, and there are many scenarios that can trigger it, causing you to fall under its spell of apathy.

Triggers for Debilitating Resistance

Overwhelmed – Sometimes you set a goal for yourself that is so important, so lofty, you become overwhelmed, either by the scope of your project, the time frame involved, the resources required, or maybe even by the personal changes you'll need to make in order to achieve your goal. Feeling too overwhelmed can trigger *debilitating resistance*.

Overloaded – Sometimes, it isn't just one big challenge that's stressing you out. Sometimes, so many little things are clamoring for your attention that sorting through them all begins to feel hopeless. Any action you take is a drop in the bucket considering everything else that still needs to be done. Becoming overloaded with too many responsibilities at once can cause *debilitating resistance* to flare up, and when it does, you shut down.

Lack of Confidence – Sometimes, it's an anticipation of failure (maybe triggered by memories of past failures) that triggers your resistance and sabotages your ability to take good, healthy actions to advance your life. Why begin doing something when, deep down, you don't believe it's going to work out?

Fear of the Unknown or Imagined – You might be afraid of taking a risk, knowing that the outcome is uncertain. (And really, all outcomes are uncertain.) You might be stuck in a negative mindset, to the extent that you are only envisioning worst-case scenarios, playing them out over and over in your head until you find yourself up against some powerful resistance.

Fear of Success – Believe it or not, you can be afraid of success because, on some level, you know that every time you accomplish a big goal in life, you set a new precedent for achievement and how you are expected to live your life going forward. On some level, you might be afraid of the new responsibilities and higher expectations that come with success. That fear, either latent or obvious, can trigger *debilitating resistance.*

Judgement and Conditioning – You might be internalizing some misplaced limitations, doubts, opinions, criticisms, or pessimism from other people. They're misplaced because they're originating outside of your own natural powers of deduction. Consequently, your confidence wavers, resistance rears its head, and you lose your ability to act in your own best interest.

Undeserved – Maybe, on some level, you don't believe you deserve what you really want in life. Maybe there's some form of internalized guilt or shame feeding your resistance and blocking your ability to go after what you really desire.

Unknown – You may have no idea what is causing your *debilitating resistance*. You just know that you're stuck in it. Maybe there are some misguided loyalties at play, or some hindering belief system embedded deep in your subconscious. Whatever the cause is, it's not serving you. What it's doing is reinforcing your resistance to making good, independent decisions for yourself.

If you suspect that any of the influences listed above are triggering your *debilitating resistance* and sabotaging your hopes and dreams in life, then take heart! There are some things you can do to reduce even the most tenacious resistance, so that you can then push through it and start accomplishing things again.

Below, I've listed some techniques that I've used to reduce my own *debilitating resistance*. These techniques are simple tricks that really do work. They won't remove all your resistance in one fell swoop, but they should begin to chip away at it until, eventually, you'll be able to push through it and get your life back on track.

Techniques for Reducing Debilitating Resistance

Make a List – By breaking down what you need to do into a manageable list that's out in front of you, you stop your thoughts about these things from bouncing around in your brain, where they are likely creating anxiety. Additionally, when your goals, along with some steps for achieving them, are written down, they become more tangible in nature and, therefore, more manageable. This should begin to reduce some of your anxiety over them, which in turn reduces your resistance. Plus, you'll get a much-needed sense of accomplishment each and every time you check another item off your to-do list!

Start an Accomplishment Journal – Journaling your accomplishments at the end of the day is immensely empowering. Even on your most sluggish days, you will have accomplished something. I don't care if it's simply washing your face and getting dressed. That's an accomplishment! Record it! Everyone responds well to having a sense of accomplishment. Believe it or not, when you have a sense of accomplishment, your brain releases chemicals that put you in a more positive state of mind. Then you can accomplish even more!

Take a Time-Out – Resistance is normal. It doesn't always have to be the Big Bad Wolf at the door. It's a natural component of a forward-moving life. Sometimes, you just need to give into it for an allotted period of time and let it play itself out. Find something else to do for a while—something you're not so resistant to. *Resistance attracts resistance.* So, resistance in one area of your life can lead to resistance in all areas of your life. The good news is that the reverse is also true: *action begets action.* So, by taking action in an area of your life that you're not so resistant to, you can begin to build up some momentum for taking action in the areas triggering resistance.

Form a Better Support System – If you're not getting the support you need and deserve from your family members, friends, colleagues, and/or acquaintances, then you have got to reduce your time spent with these people so that you can get to work establishing a more encouraging and supportive social network. Make no mistake, when others demonstrate that they have doubts or disapprove of what you are trying to do, your own self-doubt proliferates. Start looking for ways to bring more like-minded people into your life. Join clubs, organizations, or groups that attract the kinds of people you admire and resonate with. When you spend time with kindred spirits, you are endowed with their positive validation and support. That support goes a long way towards reducing the influence of those who may be projecting their own fears and limitations onto you (consequently fueling your resistance), while not necessarily having your best interests in mind.

Step Out of Your Everyday Environment – Go to the beach, mountains, countryside, or city. Go anywhere that inspires you, just as long as it's not where you are now! When you move into new environments, your energy expands. Resistance not only creates constrictive energy, it thrives in it. By doing something that brings new experiences and movement into your life, you can often break up the constrictive energy that resistance has enveloped you in.

Take Baby Steps – If you can take even one itsy-bitsy baby step towards achieving your goals, then you are still making progress. It doesn't matter that it's one step in a million you still need to take, forward is forward. Resistance doesn't want you to take any steps forward! Even one (seemingly insignificant) step a day towards your goal will begin to chip away at your resistance until, eventually, you'll be accelerating towards your goals—full steam ahead! You'll also be pleasantly surprised when you realize that all those seemingly insignificant baby steps added up to a really nice head start. You won't be starting at square one anymore!

Make a Pros and Cons List – Sometimes, resistance settles in because you haven't quite sorted things out yet. Maybe you've got some lingering doubts about what you are trying to do, and those doubts are triggering your resistance. In this kind of situation, *intuitive resistance* and *debilitating resistance* are actually two sides of the same coin. By making a pros and cons list, you will begin to better understand the matter at hand. What are the pros and cons of going after your aspirations? What are the pros and cons of not going after them? I think you'll find that once you feel more comfortable with your decisions, your resistance wanes.

Journal – I highly recommend journaling for anyone struggling with resistance of any kind. Write down everything you feel, think, fear, hate, love, want… whatever! As you identify a thought or a feeling, write it down. Don't try to keep your journal neat and proper. You're not going to publish this thing or give it to anyone else to read. Just dump your thoughts and feelings onto paper in a messy stream-of-consciousness format. Write, write, write! Write until there is nothing else you can think of to write. When your tumultuous and jumbled thoughts, fears, doubts, and concerns bounce around in your brain, over time they can coalesce into one big cloud of anxiety. You'll start to pull apart that noxious cloud as you write down everything that's clamoring for your attention. You'll be able to look at things more clearly and put them into their proper context. This technique works like a charm when it comes to reducing overall anxiety. When anxiety is reduced, so is resistance.

Do Something Creative – Let's say that you want to start up a business, but you just can't seem to pull it together enough to begin the process. Then maybe paint a picture instead. Refinish that old desk in the garage. Do a creative project that isn't part of a greater goal. This may seem like a distraction at first, but small creative projects get your creative juices flowing. Resistance blocks energy, and it blocks creative energy first and foremost. By doing little creative projects that your resistance isn't so attached to, you can begin to release a flow of creative energy into other areas of your life. Active creative energy weakens resistance!

Exercise – Go for a walk. Ride your bike. Do yoga. Go to the gym. It doesn't matter what you do, just as long as it involves some kind of amped-up physical activity. Resistance, when unmet, builds up inert, dense energy in your energy field. By moving your body and getting your physical energy moving again, you can start to break through the inert, dense energy of resistance as well.

All of the above are tried-and-true techniques for reducing the grip of *debilitating resistance*. I recommend trying them out (in any order) and experimenting with them. I think you'll find that some will work better for you than others.

That said, I have found that there is still something else you can do to help break up and then push through even the most stubborn resistance. It's something I recommend doing in combination with any of the techniques listed above, because it will make those techniques a little easier to engage in, and a little more effective once engaged.

In other words…

There's a technique you can apply to break through your resistance to the techniques you can apply to break through resistance! It's something I like to refer to as "clearing space."

Clearing Space

Clearing space is something you can do to *clear* dysfunctional, negative energy from your physical environment.

"If you want to know the secrets of the Universe, think in terms of energy, frequency and vibration." —Nikola Tesla

Have you ever walked into a room after there has been a heated argument there? You can sometimes feel that there has been an incident, even if you weren't personally present to witness it. It's like some form of residual anger still lingers in the air, causing the room to feel heavy and thick for a time.

Well, imagine, if you will, that your *debilitating resistance* is a thick, sticky energy being generated first and foremost by your own thoughts and emotions. You already know that your resistance is affecting your ability to take certain actions in your life, but it could be affecting your physical environment as well. Some form of that thick, sticky energy could be lingering in your physical space, just like angry energy can linger in a room after an argument.

By taking certain actions to "clear space," you can begin to "clear" the thick, sticky energy of resistance that might be attached to your physical environment.

Once cleared, your physical environment can no longer work in tandem with whatever else is going on in your life to compound your resistance.

So, how exactly do you *clear space*?

There are many methods and rituals out there for clearing negative energy from your environment. But two of the most powerful are also the most common. You've already done both of them many times over! They are the actions of *changing* and *cleaning* your space.

Clearing through Changing

If all things are fundamentally comprised of energy, then as you *change* something about your environment, you subsequently *change* the energy in your environment. As you *change* the energy in your environment, you *clear* energy from your environment, because all things *changed* have shed (and, therefore, *cleared*) something of their old selves.

When you clear space, by changing something about your space, you introduce a new vibe into that space. That new energy will begin to displace some of the old, stale energy of resistance.

You can change the energy in your space by rearranging the items in your space. You can also do it by introducing more light or a different color scheme. You can also do it by repairing, organizing, altering, or enhancing something about your space. And, you can change your space by moving into another space entirely, or by changing something about yourself. You are, after all, your own space!

Clearing space, by changing something about your space, can be fun to do! It gets your creative juices flowing. Active, creative energy reduces resistance!

110

Clearing through Cleaning

When you *clean*, you stir up and *clear* out old, stale energy as you eliminate dirt, filth, and disorder from your space. *Cleaning*, therefore, is another way to *clear* any old, stale energy of resistance that might be attached to your environment.

Cleaning includes actual cleaning, of course, but it can also include decluttering, organizing, and discarding what doesn't fit or work in your life anymore.

You can clear the old, stale energy of resistance from your space by cleaning your space because, as you clean, you address the stuff that old, stale energy is attached to.

Clearing Affects Your Mind

Clearing space (by cleaning and/or changing something about your space) not only affects your environment, it also affects your mind.

You internalize your surroundings by observing and experiencing your surroundings. Therefore, it stands to reason that, as you work to clear resistant energy from your surroundings, by virtue of your observation and experience while clearing, you can begin to clear some of your internalized resistant thinking as well.

Clearing Affects Your Feelings

Clearing space (by cleaning and/or changing something about your space) not only affects your environment, it also affects your emotions.

Cleared space feels light. Resistance feels heavy. These two feelings can't coexist because they're dichotomous. Therefore, when you spend time in space that feels lighter, you begin to feel less resistant.

Intention

Clearing space is a highly effective tool for dispelling any resistance that might be attached to your living environment. That said, when you combine the act of clearing space with *intention*, then you can identify and direct the new energy you want to come into your space, so you don't end up reestablishing the same old, resistant energy that had you so stuck in the first place.

Whenever you clear space, you can "intend" for the new energy coming into that space to be more conducive to your goals.

Below, I've included an example of how this might work in a relatively common scenario:

Unemployment

Let's say that you've been laid off from work and need to find another job, but you just can't seem to get out of bed in the morning to go on another disappointing interview. Your enthusiasm and confidence are at an all-time low. For all essential purposes, you're paralyzed by your resistance. This would be the perfect time to shift your focus off job hunting for a time, and refocus it on clearing space instead.

Before filling out another dreaded application, or scheduling another disastrous interview, you might want to clean out your closet instead, all the while intending that your remaining wardrobe will be more reflective of a successful career person's life. You might want to get rid of anything that doesn't fit you properly, or isn't in good condition, because a *bad fit* or *poor condition* no longer represents who you want to be. You might also want to give your house a good cleaning. Maybe clean out the kitchen pantry, and the refrigerator while you're at it. Consider changing your bedding, making sure that your new sheets are crisp and clean, and that your bed is attractively dressed—inviting sleep. You might also want to do something different with your hair. Maybe get a new cut and style for the new you.

All of this might seem beside the point—and that's exactly the point. You've pulled your attention away from finding a new job (temporarily) and refocused it on clearing space instead, which is not so threatening to the part of you that is resisting. In addition, you've been able to do all of this with the *intention* that your new space will be more compatible with your goal of finding a job.

One of the beautiful things about clearing space is that you don't have to address the whole of your resistance head-on to work up some momentum for pushing through it.

Now, the next time you go shopping, you'll want to put healthier, more energizing food in your pantry and refrigerator. When you go to bed at night, you'll feel better slipping between those clean, crisp sheets. You'll sleep better at night, and you'll wake up feeling more refreshed in the morning. You'll have more confidence as you dress in more attractive clothing and comb your newly styled hair into place. You'll feel better about your life in general because you'll feel better about the space you're living, resting, and planning your life from.

By *clearing space* (by *changing* and/or *cleaning* your space), you've shifted the energy in your space. You've invited *fresh and new* energy into your space, which is counteracting the stale, old energy of resistance. And, you've been able to do all of this with the *intention* of finding a new job!

Ultimately, you should feel better about yourself and perform better at your next job interview. And, before you know it, you'll be feeling better and performing better at your brand-new job!

Smudging

Smudging is a ritualistic act that uses smoke from sacred herbs and oils to clear and sanctify space.

Numerous cultures and religions from around the world and throughout history have used some form of smudging to clear and sanctify space.

Because smudging is partly spiritual in nature, I hesitated to include it in this book. I know that folks will have their own views on all things spiritual. Let me just say that clearing space by simply cleaning and/or changing your space (without smudging) is effective! You don't have to smudge.

Personally, I smudge. I find it works for me. I always give the area I'm going to smudge a good cleaning and decluttering first. That way, I start the process off in a space that feels clearer from the get-go.

I typically use white sage when I smudge. My process is fairly simple. Feel free to investigate various smudging techniques and go with one that resonates with you. Most will be more involved than what I'm sharing with you here.

I start by saying a prayer. Then I light the sage. Then I slowly walk around my space, filling it with smoke and saying out loud, "By the Love of God, Light of God, and Grace of God, I ask that this place be cleared of all negative influences, imprints, thoughts forms, attachments, and energies." After I've walked through the entire space, saying those words and filling it with smoke, I return to my starting point and do it again. Only this time I say, "With the Love of God, Light of God, and Grace of God, I ask that this space be filled and blessed." Then I do the whole process a third time, saying, "By the Love of God, Light of God, and Grace of God, I ask that this space be protected, and that all harmful and negative influences be kept out." That's it. It's that simple. Yet based on my experience, it's greatly effective!

Perhaps one of the nicest things about smudging is that it gives you back a sense of personal power over your environment. Let's face it, we are constantly being bombarded with conditions and energies we wouldn't choose for ourselves. It's empowering to engage in a tangible act that sets a better intention for your living space, while at the same time asking for some divine assistance.

The Butterfly Totem

In the beautiful and mystical town of Sedona, it's not uncommon to overhear people talking about their animal totems. The idea that animals can act as representatives who convey messages, guidance, and protection from the spirit world is an ancient one. It's steeped in the traditions of ancient people who walked this land many years ago, and it's still a tradition recognized by many living today.

When an animal acts as your totem, it has an important message for you. That message is often associated with the unique characteristics of the animal itself.

Today, I would like to highlight the butterfly totem, because I think it's the perfect symbolism for anyone *starting over* in their life. One interpretation of the butterfly totem is that it's a harbinger of change and transformation. The butterfly suggests that, even though you may feel small today, and even though you may walk lowly and slowly with your little caterpillar legs today, your inherent destiny is to metamorphize into another being entirely. The butterfly reminds you that your ultimate destiny is one of beauty, flight, and purpose.

The butterfly promises that, if you can cast off your old ways, and if you can push through the tenacious resistance of your chrysalis, then you will emerge with new wings and a higher calling in life.

While the caterpillar's endless hunger consumes and taxes the flora of its world, the butterfly's free and expressive flight benefits those same life-forms when it serves as their pollinator.

You too will serve your world better once you let go of old ways and rise to a higher calling.

Have you ever watched a butterfly wiggle and claw its way out of its chrysalis? It can be an agonizing thing to behold. The butterfly struggles so much during its emergence that everything in you wants to interfere and help it break free from that thing! But the butterfly's ability to use its new wings is directly tied to the muscle it develops as it pushes against the resistance of its chrysalis. If the butterfly doesn't struggle, the butterfly can't fly properly. The same holds true for us.

When we can meet the challenge of our resistance and go on to achieve our greater aspirations in life, we develop the skills and confidence we need to sustain those achievements.

The Choice

It's an inescapable truth that success in life comes hand in hand with resistance. And actually, if you examine the lives of highly functioning people, I think you'll find that one of the ways they can be differentiated is by their ability to stand up to and persevere through their resistance.

When you seek to live a life of relevance and purpose, then you must expect your challenges with resistance to be a lifelong dynamic.

The choice is ultimately yours to make. Only you can decide if you want to settle for a life of familiarity, consumption, and survival, or whether you will rise to something more. If you choose the latter, then you must be prepared to encounter and push through your resistance, and you must be prepared to do it time and time again. It is my hope that you can choose the latter, because I believe it's the choice that leads to your most expressive life, and ultimately your most fulfilling life. And surely, that is where the sweetest nectar lies.

Saboteurs

Chapter Eight

So, there you are. You're going about your life. You're finding your way. You're making plans and seeing results. You're grateful. You're hopeful. You've stepped into a better story and have pushed through some powerful resistance. You're on a roll… and then—BAM! What just happened? Sabotage! That's what happened! It came out of left field and now threatens to derail your perfectly attainable hopes and dreams, if you let it.

Believe it or not, most sabotage is self-inflicted.

"Nothing will sabotage our happiness and success more thoroughly than the fear that we are not enough." —Bill Crawford

In Chapter Four, "Hope," there is a discussion about the type of self-sabotage that rises out of discouragement, doubts, setbacks, insecurities, and basically anything that causes your hope to wane. That chapter then goes on to introduce the benefits of making plans, revisiting those plans, and adjusting those plans as circumstances shift and change, and then enduring and continuing to move forward with your plans, even when hope wanes. In Chapter Seven, "Resistance," self-sabotage is discussed in relation to the resistance it causes, along with some

119

helpful tips for reducing your resistance so that you can finally push through it.

The Saboteur

This chapter, however, isn't going to be about self-sabotage so much. It's going to be about a rarer, albeit formidable, type of sabotage. One that is brought about by a specific type of person: *the saboteur.*

The saboteur is someone who is deliberate, manipulative, and experienced in their attempts to undermine you.

At some point on your *starting over* journey, it's likely that a saboteur will show up and try to derail your progress. I don't want to frighten you with this probability; I want to warn you.

Forewarned is forearmed.

That said, just as there are techniques for dealing with the types of self-sabotage that result from *waning hope* and *debilitating resistance*, there are proven ways to deal with a saboteur as well.

Vulnerability

Trust me when I say that *starting over* is going to take you through a *period of discovery*. That's an exciting time when you get to experiment with new scenarios as you pick and choose ways to better *harmonize what you do with who you are*. That said, with experimentation comes a degree of vulnerability, and it's going to be your vulnerability that could open you up and draw in the attention of a saboteur.

Like a moth to a flame, saboteurs are attracted to the vulnerability of those trying to improve their lives.

Let's make sure that you can recognize saboteurs for who they are, early enough in your dealings with them, so you can effectively shut them down. You don't want to underestimate these people. And, you certainly don't want your best possible future highjacked because of the games and contentions they bring to the table.

You have every right, and indeed a responsibility, to shut down saboteurs and their disruptive behaviors so that you can continue doing what you're meant to be doing with your life.

Difficult People

Difficult people are around us all the time. At any given time, you can spot the critics, naysayers, braggarts, gossips, controllers, snobs, micromanagers, complainers, mimics, liars, pretenders, aggressors, users, moochers, competitors, perpetual victims, overachievers, underachievers, people who are way too serious, people who aren't serious enough... and the list goes on! Difficult people are one of the reasons you will need your personal mantra of defiance. They present challenges that require you to step into your *"So FN what!"* stance and declare, "I'm going to make this work!"

ALL OF US ARE DIFFICULT PEOPLE in one way or another, and at one time or another. Right! We all have our idiosyncrasies, and they're not always pleasant for others to experience. That said...

While all of us have our difficult moments to contend with, and all of us can make life difficult for others at times, not all of us predictably rise to the level of sabotage. Saboteurs do.

Naïveté

I don't recall knowing any saboteurs in my childhood. None of my family members were saboteurs, and neither were any of my friends, teachers, neighbors, nor anyone else I was aware of. My lack of experience with these people was a blessing on the one hand, but it also meant that I grew up rather naïve to their existence. When I did finally move out on my own, and I started to encounter these people for the first time, I was the proverbial deer in headlights! I had no idea what I was up against or how to handle them! As saboteurs began occasionally crossing my path, it took decades of me responding with displays of exasperation and outrage (usually to my detriment) before I finally learned the *right* (that is, *effective*) way of dealing with them.

Today, thankfully, I'm not so naïve. Today, I tend to recognize these people early on in my dealings with them because I've come to recognize that they all share many of the same characteristics. That's welcome insight because...

The sooner you can recognize that you are dealing with a saboteur, the sooner you can take certain actions to mitigate their potentially damaging effects in your life.

The Eighteen Characteristics

Now, let me just say that I have zero experience in the fields of psychiatry, psychology, or any of their subdisciplines. I'm pretty sure that if any of these trained professionals were to look at my list of characteristics for a saboteur, they would say something like, "Oh, you're talking about such-and-such disorder." The designation of *saboteur* is simply my layperson's way of identifying a type of person who consistently and predictably sabotages the life experiences of others. In other words, sabotage is a way of life for this person. It's how they get it done, so to speak.

I also think it's important to note that ALL OF US will exhibit some of these characteristics from time to time. I don't want to come across as too self-righteous or judgmental here because, even as I was writing these down, I recalled occasions when I was doing some of this same sort of stuff (sadly), like embellishing or being overly disruptive. You'll probably recognize yourself in some of these as well. That said, exhibiting one or two of these characteristics occasionally doesn't denote a saboteur. It's certainly nothing to be proud of, but it doesn't make you a true saboteur. Remember, saboteurs use sabotage as a way of life. It's their path to power. That means they will exhibit more of these characteristics (if not all of them), and they will do so predictably.

Below, I've listed eighteen characteristics that I've come to recognize in the type of person I'm calling a true saboteur:

1. **They self-appoint themselves into positions of authority.** Saboteurs want to be in control. They often insert themselves into authoritative roles (such as managers, supervisors, directors, etc.), even when they don't have the official designation or right to do so.

2. **They brag and embellish.** Saboteurs want to be in the know about everything and everyone. They often try to one-up you. *"Anything you can do, I can do better"* seems to be a mantra of theirs. They name-drop. They brag. They make certain that you know they were successful in past endeavors. Yet if you pull back the veil and investigate some of their claims more closely, you will often find that their performance was subpar. Ei-

ther that, or some of their so-called achievements and accolades were entirely fabricated.

3. **They fixate.** Saboteurs fixate on people, things, and circumstances. They can't let go of minor annoyances the way most of us do. They have a lot of resentments and tend to spend a great amount of time and energy getting even for perceived offenses that most of us would shrug off. They fixate romantically as well. They can be controlling, manipulative, jealous, and territorial in romantic relationships. Their behavior towards perceived rivals (romantic or otherwise) can be obsessive, irrational, and destructive.

4. **They have boundary issues.** Saboteurs snoop, sneak, creep, pry, and spy. They invade personal space. If they believe that they can get away with it, they will unapologetically sidestep both ethics and laws if it serves their agenda.

5. **They gaslight.** Saboteurs love to gossip, criticize, and dish out misinformation at a perceived rival's expense. Their aim is to damage that person's reputation and reduce their social support. Saboteurs distort facts. They mix truth with fiction to muddy the waters. They often preemptively accuse others of doing the same destructive things that they themselves are doing. Because of all the confusion, misinformation, and misdirection generated, the truth isn't always going to be apparent.

6. **They gather allies.** Saboteurs are experts at gathering allies. They combine charm, identifiability, fake sincerity, and vulnerability to create attractive personas that others gravitate to at first blush. They are particularly skilled at identifying and aligning themselves with

others based on commonly held associations that their victim probably won't share (such as partying, music, hobbies, work, sports, talents, children, pets, fraternities, sororities, club memberships, socioeconomics, etc.). They also move allies into their corner rather effortlessly by bonding with them through strongly held identity factors (such as race, gender, ethnicity, politics, or religion). They are not beyond using flattery and even sexuality when it comes to gathering allies.

7. **They are disruptors.** Saboteurs are wired to disrupt preestablished dynamics and relationships. If they covet something someone else has, their first step is usually to stir up the energy in that person's environment. In other words, they stir the pot. They've learned that disruptive energy begets contention, which begets weakened alliances. They can then take advantage of those weaknesses to realign themselves into key relationships. They can change the dynamics of a situation so quickly that someone is usually left a little gobsmacked and wondering what the heck just happened!

8. **They are irrational.** Saboteurs react to triggers that you and I will never fully understand. Their emotionally charged reactions will often appear irrational. Also, because they incorporate so much manipulation and misdirection into everything they do, their actions and reactions, when taken at face value, don't always make sense.

9. **They are easily offended.** Saboteurs can rise to the level of feeling personally attacked over relatively minor events. When this happens, it doesn't matter who's right or wrong, or even what really happened. A formidable reaction (and usually retaliation) is engaged, and

it's extremely difficult (if not impossible) to get things sorted out accurately and fairly.

10. **They are self-righteous.** Saboteurs almost always project an air of self-righteousness, entitlement, and superiority. When they've done something to *get at* someone, even if it was predatory, dishonest, or cruel at the time, there is rarely any guilt or remorse expressed.

11. **They gloat.** Saboteurs gloat when they think they've outwitted someone or are about to. Their eyes will literally sparkle with self-satisfaction. They'll gloat in anticipation as well, even before it becomes apparent that they've done something nefarious. They have a coy side to them that they're really quite proud of.

12. **They defer blame.** Every bad thing that has ever happened to a saboteur will always be someone else's fault, and they have a long list of offenders. They're not capable of the self-reflection needed to understand how their own actions (or inactions) contributed to their misfortunes. Instead, they're wired to always cast blame outward. Because of this, sadly, saboteurs don't stand in their true power. They've learned instead to rely on trickery and victimhood for their successes in life. Their story to the world will often be that they are immensely smart, talented, and destined for great things, but if those great things fail to manifest, then it's because of this thing… or that thing… or that person… or those people. They won't accept that any misfortune is due to the cause and effect of their own decisions and behaviors.

13. **They can be childish.** There is often a childlike demeanor in a saboteur that surfaces from time to

time. Some will even resort to childlike mannerisms and can take on a childish voice. If you can't make sense of what they're doing or why they're doing it, try to see the child in them for a moment. What age is that child? How would a hurt, resentful child of that age behave? If you can recognize the childlike energy that is surfacing in them, then their behavior might begin to make a little more sense to you.

14. **They have a history.** If you investigate a saboteur's past, you will often discover a pattern of sabotaging behavior, evidenced by a list of strained and severed relationships. It will be a long list. Manipulating, undermining, discrediting, disrupting, deceiving, and throwing others off their game gives the saboteur a temporary sense of superiority, which they've come to rely on like a drug to feel better about themselves. It's temporary, however, because it's not based in the truth of things. Therefore, saboteurs must manipulate, undermine, discredit, disrupt, deceive, and throw others off their game over and over again to continue feeling good about themselves. Sabotage is a learned way of life for them, and it tends to leave a historical record.

15. **They are likeable.** Saboteurs are not monsters. They are real people who (I believe) have two equally relevant sides to them. On the one side, they have warm, likeable personalities, which they can rest in and present to the world on a day-to-day basis. On the other side, they are petty, obsessive, judgmental, provocative, manipulative, and vindictive when triggered. Each side is equally genuine when they are functioning in it. This duality makes them difficult to identify at first. I still (on occasion) get drawn to the more likable side of a saboteur, even knowing full well that he or she is a sab-

oteur! They are great connectors when they want to be. They've learned how to form energetic links with others in relatively short periods of time. They are experts at using eye contact with undertones of sincerity to establish trust. They can be generous to a fault if it serves their agenda.

16. **They show vulnerability.** Saboteurs have learned that their misfortunes in life (which they will rarely take personal responsibility for) can serve them by making them more relatable and by eliciting sympathy from others, which they then use to form emotional ties. When they periodically fall into bouts with depression, desperation, panic, or despair (and they do have such episodes), their vulnerability and pain will be evident. The suffering you see in them at those times will be one hundred percent real, and it can be heartbreaking to observe. But it's also manipulative. It's very hard to hold someone accountable for their behavior when they are genuinely suffering and in crisis.

17. **They are manipulative.** Saboteurs almost never play it straight—not for any length of time anyway. It's far too easy for them to convincingly lie, cheat, embellish, and change the truth of things for their own benefit. They observe people closely and look for ways to undermine them, should it become advantageous to do so. They size people up. They set people up. I once knew a woman who put stolen money in another woman's purse because she didn't like her. Fortunately, her stunt didn't work because it was caught on a security camera. Still, I shudder to think of how devastating it could have been for the innocent woman had the scheme worked.

18. **They micromanage.** Saboteurs almost always micromanage their environment. First and foremost, it gives them a sense of control, which they so desperately desire. But it also gives them ammunition for picking away at someone's confidence and reputation if they choose to. No one can possibly live up to all their rules and conditions (which they are constantly changing, by the way). So, when someone does make a mistake (and they will), the saboteur has the option to highlight that mistake in an effort to undermine that person.

These are the eighteen characteristics that I've come to recognize in the type of person I'm calling a saboteur. I know there are people with diagnosable personality disorders who exhibit some of these same characteristics (there are narcissists and sociopaths, for example). But I'm not convinced that these people will always resort to sabotage. I think they *can* resort to sabotage, certainly, if it serves them. But I'm not sure that it's a given.

A true saboteur will always and predictably resort to sabotage. It's their learned path to power.

Also, there are people who have ridiculously high opinions of themselves. They will undoubtedly exhibit some of these characteristics as well (such as superiority and self-righteousness). But again, I'm not sure that they will always resort to sabotage. And, to be perfectly honest, I don't believe that true saboteurs have high opinions of themselves. From what I've been able to observe about them, regardless of the air of superiority they project, if you observe them more closely, you will be able to detect a profoundly damaged sense of self.

Saboteurs don't believe their truth is good enough. That's why they resort to lies, trickery, interference, guilting, sham-

ing, and other forms of manipulation to get what they want in life.

Why Are They This Way?

It's my belief that people who are constantly disrupting and sabotaging the lives of others, do so because they lack a sense of self-worth, fundamentally, at their core.

When a saboteur resorts to sabotage, it's a manipulative means to rise above others so that they can feel more accomplished in themselves.

I'm guessing that sabotage became a type of coping behavior that developed when they were still quite young (hence the childlike behavior). Possibly because someone in their formative years didn't give them the value, support, guidelines, or validation they needed to develop into authentic, well-adjusted adults. I'm almost certain now that when I can identify the age of the inner child I'm seeing in a saboteur, I'm identifying the age when that person internalized some serious developmental damage.

The tragedy in all of this is: because saboteurs resort to manipulative behavior out of a sense of inadequacy, each and every time they are successful at it, they reinforce their belief that without these manipulative behaviors, they are still inadequate. It's a subconscious belief that reinforces their behavior, and their behavior reinforces the belief.

And, as if that weren't bad enough, there's another self-damning caveat linked to sabotaging behavior. Saboteurs can't be underhanded, manipulative, dishonest, and successful at sabotaging others without feeling at least a little guilty about it on some level. So, even though they shrug off remorse and guilt (and they do), and even though they will gloat like the cat who swallowed the canary (and they will), on some level, their subconscious mind is absorbing it all.

Eventually, a saboteur doesn't just have a latent belief that he or she is, deep down, inadequate, but that belief gets compounded with repressed guilt.

Just because their guilt is repressed, that doesn't mean it isn't there. Buried guilt further chips away at a saboteur's sense of self-worth.

They Deserve Compassion

I believe that, deep down, saboteurs are just wounded children who feel like they are less than everyone else around them. They are trapped in their destructive coping behaviors. Unless they can step back well enough to be reflective, and acknowledge they are trapped in a pattern of behavior that isn't serving them anymore, but is, in fact, limiting their ability to step into their real power in life, then they will always be heading towards some form of self-destruction. They need help. They need compassion. They need healing.

Saboteurs are wounded people who deserve compassion. That said, they don't have a right to exercise their destructive behavior in your life.

Why You Might Trigger a Saboteur

Because saboteurs are compensating for their own insecurities, and because they are outwardly focused on others to avoid any painful self-reflection and growth, they don't engage in the personal work needed to develop genuine self-esteem. Therefore, saboteurs live in a constant state of vulnerability to their insecurities. That's important to understand because if you are *starting over* in life, and if you are aspiring to do so consciously, then you are engaging in the self-reflection and inner work needed to live your best possible life. Your sheer gumption in doing so could attract the attention, and then the resentment of a saboteur sooner or later.

Your desire to improve your life can trigger a saboteur.

To better understand what triggers a saboteur into action, I think we should take a look at the types of people they're most likely to target.

People They Target

The Self-Improver – Self-improvers are self-reflective. They are seeking to identify and make the personal changes needed to usher better experiences into their lives (legitimately so). True saboteurs avoid this kind of responsibility like the plague. Therefore, anyone aspiring to create a better life for themselves could trigger powerful feelings of resentment in a saboteur, who is likely to respond with some form of sabotage sooner or later.

The Optimist – Optimists see possibilities. They are lighthearted by nature. The one thing saboteurs are not is lighthearted. Not really. They can certainly put on a show to try to appear that way. Saboteurs love to emulate optimists. But in their heart of hearts, they're pessimists. They've given up on their real hopes and dreams and are no longer in touch with their authentic selves. In that sense, they are walking down a compromised life path, which generates pessimism, not optimism. Therefore, an optimist will trigger resentment in a saboteur by simply existing. Turning a positive person negative is a great source of victory for a saboteur. It's like a drug that restores their sense of personal power.

The Innocent – Innocence will annoy a saboteur. True saboteurs lost their innocence ages ago and don't value it anymore anyway. In fact, they've come to view innocence as folly. Taking advantage of someone's innocence is seen as an opportunity by a saboteur. It gives them a chance to feel superior to their victims, which in turn reinforces their false narrative that they are superior to most people in general.

The Vulnerable – A saboteur targets the vulnerable in two ways. First, they can take on the role of a bully. That's when they'll attack someone who isn't likely to get a lot of support, just because they can. It's easy to do, and it gives their floundering ego the temporary illusion of strength. But there is a second, more insidious way that they will target the vulnerable. When a saboteur identifies someone who is overly shy, or who lacks self-esteem, or who feels marginalized in their environment in some way, they might offer that person attention and support, thereby gaining an ally. They aren't doing this out of kindness, however. In fact, they've already identified some weaknesses and flaws in the person and will be harboring some cloaked judgements of them from the get-go. No, a saboteur's support for a vulnerable person is typically transactional at its root. It may not be evident at first, but there's a hidden agenda behind it. This is a particularly damaging strategy because saboteurs can abruptly pull their support from anyone who stops serving their needs. When that happens, an already vulnerable individual, who so desperately relished the recognition and support they were receiving for a time, can be left even more damaged by the ultimate judgement, abandonment, and betrayal.

The Enemy – Regardless of the charismatic and confident personality they present to the world, saboteurs are insecure, hypersensitive, and always on the lookout for enemies. An enemy can be someone who has offended them (which isn't hard to do), or a competitor. It can also be someone who has something they want. An enemy can also be someone living their life in such a way that the saboteur is reminded of what he or she doesn't have the guts to do. Saboteurs will also have adversarial relationships with anyone (including family members, children, partners, friends, and even pets!) who plays a supportive role in the life of someone they are trying to influence. Once a saboteur identifies an enemy, they are tenacious, coy, manipulative, sneaky, covert, and overt at chipping away at that entity's value, credibility, and reputation.

People They Don't Target

Those in Charge – Saboteurs are skilled manipulators. Therefore, they're quite clever when it comes to self-preservation. They recognize the hand that feeds them. So, even if they don't really like the person in charge at the time, they will be able to pull off compliance, flattery, and even servitude if they think that person has control over their destiny. They will do their best to be an irreplaceable asset to that person.

Those They Admire – Saboteurs recognize kindred spirits. They can become downright smitten with people who operate in much the same way that they do. They study such people. They admire such people. They often look up to them.

Those Who Give Them Unconditional Support – Saboteurs desperately need to feel admired. They need people around them who will shore up and validate their more favorable persona. They can't resist enablers who offer them support without challenging them too much. (Although they will also harbor some contempt for their enablers.) Without such people in their lives, saboteurs can sink into bouts with depression. Their strong need for admiration also makes them susceptible to other manipulators who are willing to offer them these things to get something in exchange. Sadly, many saboteurs have sacrificed beautiful relationships with genuine people who truly loved them, because they were enamored with and placated for a time by another saboteur.

The Key to Handling Them

The key to handling a saboteur lies in a universal truth, which, by the way, happens to be the key to handling most of life's disruptive events. And that is…

What you put your attention and actions into ultimately decides your fate in life.

I think most of us know this truth already. But having it so integrated into our consciousness that we automatically respond by it takes some intention and practice. Case in point:

The Neighborhood Saboteur

(Note: Some of the names and details in this narrative have been changed out of respect for the individuals involved.)

135

When I was still in the early days of building up my real estate business in the town of Sedona, I was lucky enough to secure a listing in my own neighborhood. The house was down the street from mine, and it was owned by a woman named Kelly.

I put a lot of effort into selling Kelly's house. I personally helped her clean, paint, and stage her house. I went above and beyond what is typically done for a listing because I knew that the sale of this house, however it went, would hit our neighborhood's grapevine like the speed of light, and my reputation as a real estate agent (at least in my own backyard) would either be made or ruined. I was focused and excited about selling this house!

Enter the neighbor…

One afternoon, as I was walking down the street on my way to drop off some extra brochures at Kelly's house, Sue, another neighbor of ours, came off her front porch and joined me at the sidewalk for a bit of a chat. After a moment or two of polite conversation, she brought up my listing. She said that she had noticed I had Kelly's house up for sale, and she wanted to warn me about Kelly's next-door neighbor, Tim. She said that she was pretty sure Tim was training his two dogs for illegal dog fighting. When I asked her how she knew about this, she admitted that she didn't have any real proof, other than this was what she had heard from her friends in the Ladies Bridge Club. Her friends' beliefs about Tim and his dogs, and the fact that she herself had seen some pretty shady characters coming and going from Tim's house, was all the proof she needed to believe it was true. She went on to say that she believed I was going to have a hard time selling Kelly's house because of all the *goings-on* next door. She warned me to be careful, wished me luck, and then returned to her front porch.

I was planning on holding an open house at Kelly's house that Sunday (which was why I had the extra brochures) and, I must admit, after this brief encounter with Sue, I was starting to feel a little apprehensive about it. Could the rumors about Tim be true? I hadn't personally seen or heard anything suspicious going on at his house.

I called Kelly (who had moved out of the area) from my cell phone as I continued down the street towards her house. I told her about my conversation with Sue. Kelly responded by saying that she wasn't aware of the rumors. She told me that she knew Tim and his dogs quite well, and she assured me that the rumors were false. She went on to say that she considered Tim to be a good neighbor. After talking with her, I felt better about the whole situation, but I was also committed to paying closer attention to Tim's house in an attempt to better understand the truth of things.

As I walked up Kelly's driveway, Tim must have spotted me from inside of his house because he came to his front door and waved. I waved back. So far, so good. I went inside Kelly's house, placed the brochures on her kitchen counter, and decided to venture out into the backyard to water some plants. Also, I wanted to see if Tim's dogs were outside because I wanted to try to get a closer look at them.

The dogs were indeed outside. These two beautiful black labs were quietly watching me from their side of the fence. Once we made eye contact, the dogs got excited and began to whine and scamper back and forth along the fence line, their tails wagging enthusiastically. They certainly seemed friendly enough, so I decided to walk over to the fence and try to interact with them a bit. Sure enough, I was able to give them lots rubs and scratches behind their ears.

Eventually, Tim came out into his backyard and introduced me to his dogs properly. Their names were Pepper and Spice. They really were these bouncy, friendly sweethearts once you got to know them. I was pretty sure now that they weren't being trained to be fighting dogs. Tim gave me his cell phone number. He went on to say that if his dogs were ever to become bothersome during one of my showings, all I had to do was call or text him, and he would bring them inside. He also volunteered to water Kelly's plants in the future. What nice, neighborly gestures!

After closing up Kelly's house, I started to walk back home, feeling greatly relieved over the whole next-door neighbor situation, Sue came off her front porch and intercepted me at the sidewalk again. She mentioned that she had observed me talking with Tim, and wondered if everything was okay. I assured her that it was. I was going to wish her a good day and leave it at that, but for some reason I added, "You know, Tim really is a nice guy once you get to know him."

Her reaction struck me as a little odd at the time. Instead of showing relief (after all, she had just expressed concern for my welfare), she pinched her lips together and didn't say anything for a moment or two. Then, finally, she responded rather dryly, "Oh, I see." Then she turned away without so much as a goodbye and walked back to her porch. I remember being somewhat perplexed by her response at the time, but I also had a lot on my mind, so I brushed it off as a peculiarity and continued back to my own house.

You see, Tim wasn't a saboteur (although initially I feared he might be). It was Sue who would turn out to be the neighborhood's saboteur. And she started to apply her finely honed skill of sabotage the moment she approached me on the sidewalk and volunteered some negative gossip about Tim, tainting my opinion of him before I had even met him. That's what they do. Right? Think about it. One of their hallmark characteristics is to stir up energy. Once Sue learned that her first attempt to stir the pot had failed, and that things were, in fact, still amicable between Tim and me, she was fully triggered. And sabotage she did!

The first thing Sue did was report Tim's dogs to the HOA. She claimed that the dogs were vicious and a danger to the community. According to Tim, an association member personally came out to his house to investigate his dogs. Tim informed me that the complaint had been dismissed because his dogs were determined to be *"compliant with the association's rules and regulations."*

Next came the rumor. Remember, Sue was a member of the Ladies Bridge Club. They were a close-knit group that met once a week. That meant their propinquity to one another, as well as their shared interests, would likely align them with Sue in any neighborhood dispute. It didn't take long before most of the neighborhood had heard the false rumor about Tim and his fighting dogs, and I have no doubt that Sue and her friends at the Ladies Bridge Club were the originators. I called Kelly (again) to discuss the matter (poor Kelly, she really didn't deserve all this craziness), and she assured me (again) that she knew Tim and his dogs personally, and that the rumor was false.

Then came what I like to refer to as Sue's *coup de théâtre.*

Sunday arrived and it was time for Kelly's open house! It was a beautiful day—sunny yet crisp. I had a feeling that the good weather was going to draw people out of their houses and, subsequently, I was going to have a lot of activity. I started the event off by driving around the neighborhood and placing my *Open House* signs at turns and intersections to guide visitors to the event. Then I opened the house for viewing.

Things at the open house started out well enough. As expected, lots of people showed up and they were milling about the house and yard. The comments I was able to overhear from potential buyers were all positive. They liked the house. They liked the location. They liked the price. That's a winning trifecta as far as selling real estate goes! I really felt like we could get an offer in by the end of the day. And then…

As I was standing by an open window in Kelly's living room, chitchatting and answering questions from potential buyers, I casually glanced over at Tim's house and saw Sue's tan Buick pulling into his driveway. *What the…?!* I mean, seriously, what was she was up to? She hated Tim! She probably wasn't going over there for a friendly chat. I watched as Sue got out of her car and walked up to Tim's front door. Tim was standing inside his door, watching her approach. I then watched what appeared to be an argument breaking out between the two of them. Sue began waving her arms about and saying something indiscernible in a shrill voice. What I was able to discern quite well was that a couple walking up Kelly's driveway did an about-face and returned to their car parked on the street. They drove away without ever coming inside.

Eventually, Sue got back into her car, backed out of Tim's driveway, and drove away up the street towards her own house. I was relieved to see her go and went back to mingling with potential buyers. But about ten minutes later, while I was still standing by the window, I glanced out again and saw two police cars pulling into Tim's driveway. I also noticed Sue's car was now parked on the street in front of Tim's house. My assumption was that she had picked a fight with Tim and then called the police on him.

As the activity next door escalated, it sadly became the focal point of my event. Folks noticed, and they couldn't clear out fast enough. I was soon left standing alone in an empty house. I felt utterly defeated. I packed up my marketing materials, turned off the lights, locked up the house, and drove through the neighborhood collecting my signs. As I made my way back to my own house, I drove past Sue, now standing in the street in front of her house. She was surrounded by a circle of her friends and, I swear, she was positively glowing with smugness.

I, on the other hand, was in a state of disbelief. What the heck had just happened? *Why* had it happened? It all seemed so unnecessary. I had gotten to know Tim personally. He seemed like a genuinely nice guy. By all accounts, he was a helpful guy. So why was Sue relentlessly harassing him? None of this made any sense to me.

When I got home, I took a shower and drank a couple of glasses of water to try to rehydrate. For some reason, I was incredibly parched. Then I prepared to do a meditation. I needed to calm down and think more clearly. My discouragement was turning into anger. My thoughts were racing as my brain turned over the day's events, trying to make sense of everything. My body was sore and tense as well. I wanted to try to release some of that tension before I worked myself up into another health crisis. Also, I wanted to see if I could gain some sort of guidance on how to manage the situation down the street because, honestly, I had no idea what to do about it.

I remember sitting cross-legged on my couch, eyes closed, taking in some slow, deliberate, deep breaths. I tried to feel a sense of well-being entering my body with my inhales, and anger and frustration leaving my body with my exhales. It started to work because I felt myself growing more relaxed and peaceful.

At some point, my mind began drifting and I began thinking about how I might go about preparing another listing of mine, due to hit the market in a couple of weeks. At first, I figured that I was just becoming distracted, but then it dawned on me: maybe this was the guidance I was seeking? Maybe this was how I was supposed to handle the contention down the street? Maybe I was supposed to take my attention off of Sue and Tim for a time, and refocus it on my new listing instead?

Later that evening, I called Kelly to discuss the matter with her. I suggested that we let things cool off a bit down the street before scheduling another open house. She agreed. Then, shifting my focus, I popped over to Tuesday Morning to get some staging items for my new listing. I spent the following week prepping and staging my new listing. I designed all the marketing materials in advance. I entered the listing data into the MLS ahead of time so that all I had to do when it was ready to go live was to activate it.

As I busied myself with these tasks, I was aware that contention was still brewing down the street. I could tell by all the missed phone calls from neighbors, many of them from Sue herself. I didn't bother returning Sue's calls, or even listening to her voicemails. There was nothing I could do about the situation anyway. For my own peace of mind, I kept busy preparing my new listing.

At some point, the phone calls stopped, and I figured the dust had settled well enough to venture down the street and check on Kelly's house.

The first thing I noticed when I got there was how quiet everything seemed. Pepper and Spice were nowhere to be seen. Tim's blinds were closed. His house had a distinct *don't bother me* look to it. I didn't bother him. I went directly into Kelly's house, opened the windows to air it out a bit, and decided to schedule another open house for the following Sunday.

That Saturday, as I was prepping Kelly's house for Sunday's event, another neighbor of ours stopped in to say hello. She updated me on what had transpired while I had been absent. She told me that Sue and Tim had gotten into another altercation (of course they did!). Various neighbors got involved and took sides (yep, I could have guessed that). The police showed up again (oh, brother), only this time, a commanding officer accused Sue of making frivolous complaints. He threatened to charge her with such if she continued calling them. After that, everything calmed down. Wow, I guess karma really does exist! Sometimes, you just have to wait for it!

That Sunday, I held another open house at Kelly's house, and it went fabulously well! Tim's dogs were in the back yard this time, and they didn't present a problem. (And actually, they had never presented a problem!) Everything was delightfully peaceful during the event—inside and out! The next day, we received a full-price offer on Kelly's house! Two weeks later, my new listing went live, and it too went under contract within its first week of being listed!

It Finally Clicked

Stepping back from the situation between Sue and Tim was a bit counterintuitive for me. Typically, I would have jumped into the fray of things and fought it out with these people. I would have tried to make sure that everyone knew the right and wrong of the situation, and I would have tried to fix everything.

The fact that I handled things differently this time around was pivotal in my understanding of how saboteurs operate—and perhaps even more importantly, how to respond to them.

This time, I didn't contend with anyone. This time, I pulled my attention away from what I couldn't control, and redirected it onto what I could control, and what would serve everyone better in the long run. I may have understood this strategy (of redirecting my attention) on some level before our neighborhood brouhaha, but after experiencing the success of it on this occasion, I got it! I mean, I intrinsically got it!

The greatest power saboteurs wield is their ability to pull you off your better trajectory in life and occupy your time and attention with the contentions they create.

My First Go-To Strategy

Today, when I find myself starting to get entangled in the web a saboteur weaves, my first go-to strategy is to remove myself from their presence and refocus my attention on something more productive. There's usually a period of time when they accelerate their antics in an attempt to pull me back into their sticky trap (like the multiple phone calls from Sue). But, if their energy continues to be unmet by mine, then, after a time, they tend to move on, and I'm able to move on as well. Hopefully undamaged in the areas of life that really matter to me.

Saboteurs thrive in contentious environments. When their disruptive tactics are not reciprocated in the manner they've become accustomed to, they tend to move on to someone or something else.

This strategy of taking time and attention away from a saboteur and redirecting it onto something more productive *almost* always works, but it doesn't *always* work. Some-times, other strategies need to be employed.

The Six Strategies

I have come to rely on six strategies for handling the saboteurs who occasionally cross my path, which I'm sharing with you below. These strategies involve specific actions that you can take to diffuse a saboteur's negative behavior, while at the same time staying focused on your better goals in life. That's important because saboteurs love to waylay you from achieving your life goals. Therefore, because you are at such a critical juncture in your life, it's imperative that you don't allow them to succeed.

1. **Refocus** – The first thing you should always do when you find yourself caught up in a saboteur's antics is remove yourself from their energy and find something else to focus on for a time. Do this immediately if you can! Stay out of their space. Stay away from their friends and acquaintances (to the degree that you can). Don't follow them on social media. Don't seek to know what they are doing. Instead, identify some greater goal or task that will directly benefit you, and put your time and attention there.

   If you can sidestep a saboteur's distraction, which is not serving you, and refocus your attention on a task that better serves you, then you will continue to move closer to your long-term goals.

2. **Be Cool** – Don't overreact. When you are emotional, you fuel a saboteur's energy, while at the same time exhausting your own. Don't give a saboteur your emotional energy. Just don't. If you can remain cool, calm,

and collected, then your energy will build up again, whereas theirs will start to diminish. Saboteurs start out slow with their antics as they test the waters, then they escalate. So, from the very first moment you suspect you might be dealing with a saboteur, reduce your interactions with him or her to necessary and polite only. Don't give them any opportunities to escalate with you if you can avoid it.

Don't give saboteurs your emotional energy. Reduce your time spent with them so that you reduce their opportunities to disrupt your life.

3. **Clarify** – Although you should never become overly preoccupied with a saboteur—ever—you may have to contend with one from time to time. When a saboteur pushes things to the point where you can't ignore them anymore, then be prepared to clarify yourself. Start by taking notes. Keep a journal of sabotaging events. Document times and dates. Do this so that you can remember the nuances and have a clearer picture of the dynamics at play, and also so that facts don't get distorted when saboteurs attempt to play the victim and distort the facts (which they will do). Most people respond to saboteurs by immediately reacting to them, but not by preparing. So, claim the advantage and be prepared. Saboteurs won't expect that. If someone else gets pulled into their drama (and they probably will), then calmly, and with facts in hand, clarify the situation. If you need to clarify yourself to an authority figure, then state your experience sincerely and factually. Keep it brief.

There may be times when you will have to contend with a saboteur by exposing their activity and clarifying the reality of events. When you do, remain factual, calm, and brief. Don't let your emotions contribute to the problem. Let the saboteur's actions and reactions remain the focal point.

4. **Keep Secrets** – When you find yourself in the direct path of a saboteur, shift immediately to being more secretive about your actions, plans, and goals in life. Keep things to yourself for a while. Don't share your plans with anyone who doesn't need to know about them, especially people who might have ties to the saboteur. If you do this effectively enough, the saboteur might become a bit unnerved. If this happens, it's because they sense something going on in your life that they can't quite pinpoint. That's okay! Keep them guessing!

   Keep actively pursuing your goals in life, but remain mysterious about them for a while! Don't share too much. This strategy will protect your energy as you move forward with your projects.

5. **Stay Engaged and Impeccable** – Although you should always seek to limit your exposure to a saboteur, you shouldn't withdraw from life in general. When a saboteur has you in their scope, it's important that you stay socially and professionally engaged, even if it's a bit forced for a while.

   Remain friendly. Remain helpful. Stay engaged in life. Remember that saboteurs love to chip away at reputations, so do everything you can to keep yours impeccable.

6. **Move On** – If the environment you are in is rewarding a saboteur, then you might not be in the right environ-

147

ment to succeed. If you find yourself in a situation like this, step back for a moment and take a good, hard look at your surroundings. Consider if moving on might be in order. At this stage in your life, success is not so dependent on winning at schoolyard games. You need to stand up for yourself to a point, yes, but your greater success in life will hinge on harmonizing who you are with the appropriate environment to succeed in. If a saboteur is being coddled by your environment, then it's probably the wrong environment for you!

Sometimes, running up against a saboteur and discovering that others are supporting him or her is a sign. It's the Universe's way of telling you that you are in the wrong place to succeed!

Other Types of Sabotage

In life, bad things happen all the time that don't necessarily involve true saboteurs. Difficult people may not be true saboteurs in the sense that they always and predictably resort to sabotage, but they can still sabotage you and create unnecessary problems. Situational events (such as storms or economic events) can stop you in your tracks and consume enormous amounts of your time and energy to work through. The simple fact is: life is always throwing curveballs.

The good news is that, even when you are dealing with other types of sabotage, many of the strategies will still work. In particular, the strategy of refocusing your attention on what you can control and what serves you, versus on what you can't control and what isn't serving you, will go a long way in getting things back on track.

When You Are the Saboteur

Have you ever thrown someone off their game? Cast shade on someone's rosy disposition? Caused an unnecessary disruption in someone's life? Well, join the club! We've all done it. We're all human, and we all have our moments. Life itself does it. You're not alone in this, and you're not a saboteur just because you're disruptive at times. The difference is that true saboteurs have adopted sabotage as a way of life. Their path to power is sabotage. That said, even though you may not be a true saboteur...

You always come from a place of insecurity when you seek to sabotage others.

When you are outwardly focused on someone else to the point of sabotaging them, then you are not focused on the right things to improve your own life. In that sense, you are sabotaging yourself. When you are triggered enough to resort to sabotaging someone, or even when you catch yourself acting in such a way that you are collaterally sabotaging someone, then you can still apply the strategies to yourself! You can take your focus off the thoughts and behaviors that are destructive (to yourself or to others) and refocus your attention on real ways to improve your own life. Your ego might take a bit of a hit at the time, but so what? In the end, your sense of accomplishment (the permanent stuff, not the temporary fix) will start to grow as you start making real progress in life.

When Not to Use the Strategies

I believe there are basically four cornerstones that serve as anchors in the foundation of every fully lived life. They are your *relationships*, *health*, *finances*, and *personal truth*.

When these four cornerstones are present and in a state of well-being, they are your assets. They support everything else you are trying to accomplish. If one of them is lacking, however, or experiencing a problem that's begging for your attention, then do yourself a big favor and attend to it. Carve out the necessary time and attention to do so. Don't use the strategies when your cornerstones are involved. Why? Because the strategies are meant to undermine, diminish, and ultimately remove something from your life. You don't want to undermine, diminish, or remove any part of your support system. You don't want to create fractures in the foundation of your life due to neglect.

If your life is lacking well-being in any of its foundational cornerstones (relationships, health, finances, or personal truth), then you will be lacking an element of support. You will be handicapped at whatever else you try to accomplish. In that respect, you will be sabotaging yourself.

The Ultimate Goal

Your future sense of accomplishment is the most important thing in the world right now, so try to keep your focus there.

Keep channeling your time and energy into ways to better "harmonize what you do with who you are." Seek out people, places, and things that resonate with your spirit. That should be your ultimate goal right now.

Don't waste any more time or energy worrying about what a saboteur is doing. Energy follows thought, so choose to hold onto your energy instead. Stay focused on your own best future. Saboteurs will expend an enormous amount of energy and attention on you. That's okay. Let them! If you apply the strategies and they still win, then you are probably not in an environment where you can realize your best possible future. Trust the Universe in this and consider moving on.

I can say with one hundred percent certainty that every time a saboteur has succeeded at separating me from something I thought I wanted, and I was able to hold onto my optimism and stay focused on my greater hopes and plans in life, I ended up evolving into better place. Each and every time! There are no exceptions to this. Conversely, the saboteur stayed exactly where I had been, stuck in a substandard position in life that really wasn't that satisfying.

Refusing to get sidetracked from your better future is the only surefire way to win at the games saboteurs play.

Section Three:
Wealthy, Healthy,
Authenic & True

Wealth
Practicalities
WRENS
Truth

Wealth

Chapter Nine

What is your truest measure of wealth? Is it your net worth? Is it how influential or respected you are in your community? Perhaps your wealth is defined in some manner by your heredity, title, degree, or some other designation bestowed upon you in life? How about your stuff? Do your clothes, jewelry, cars, real estate, or enterprises denote your wealth?

If you look at Merriam-Webster's definition for wealth, you'll find it being defined as *"having an abundance of valuable material possessions or resources."* Then there is a secondary definition: an *"abundant supply"* (of something). That would certainly explain some of our other uses for the word, such as *"She has a wealth of talent"* or *"He has a wealth of ideas."*

And then there's this explanation of wealth:

> *"Wealth is the ability to fully experience life."*
> —*Henry David Thoreau*

The True and Proper Spirit

Being able to *fully experience life* (as Henry David Thoreau so eloquently defines wealth) is what I believe to be the true and proper spirit behind any of our other concepts of wealth, because it is the ultimate reason for wealth. Why would anyone seek to acquire anything in abundance if doing so diminished their life experience?

If the true purpose behind wealth is to provide you with an ability to fully experience life, then wouldn't a truer measure of your wealth be in the realization of a fully experienced life?

The Disassociation (as pertains to material wealth)

Whenever you want to do something really big or significant in your life, I bet one of the first questions you tend to ask yourself is *What will it cost?* or perhaps *Where will the money come from?* There's nothing wrong with this tendency because in today's currency-based world, in all but the rarest of situations, your financial resources are going to be tied to your ability to live and live well. To think otherwise would be unrealistic. That said…

When you disassociate from your greater objectives in life—that is, when you put all your attention on wealth itself, at the expense of what wealth should be there to serve in your life—you lose sight of your higher callings. Then you're not fully experiencing your life anymore.

How many personal relationships, families, principles, hopes, and dreams have you seen sacrificed by those attempting to gain and hold onto material wealth? My guess is: it's quite a lot!

What about the environment? How often do we, as consumers (and oh-so-loyal constituents), allow our governments, municipalities, and corporations to run roughshod over the health and well-being of our land, knowing full well that it will be our beloved children, grandchildren, and great grandchildren who will inherit the damage? All because some immediate accumulation of wealth became paramount to these entities, and we have grown accustomed to supporting their agendas, regardless of their abuse and exploitation.

The disassociation from what wealth is meant to serve, as well as the obsessive focus on the accumulation of wealth for wealth's sake, demonstrates a dysfunctional relationship with wealth. And, as in all dysfunctional relationships, some form of abuse usually follows.

Conflicts with Material Wealth

Many of us, regardless of the degree of material wealth we may or may not have in our lives at the time, will experience some form of conflict with our material wealth. It commonly occurs when something rattles our sense of financial security so much that we become overly fixated on material wealth (or the lack thereof), often at the expense of other important things in our lives—things our wealth should be there to support, but not dominate or replace in any way.

Conflicts with material wealth are ridiculously easy to fall into because they are byproducts of our insecurities. And we all have those! Unfortunately, these conflicts distract us from realizing other important things—things we came into this world to experience and do.

Conflicts with wealth can block the healthy flow of wealth, so that wealth then fails to become the tool it's meant to be for serving some greater good.

Below, I've identified the five common conflicts that I've observed in people struggling with their material wealth. Personally, I've experienced the gamut of these at one time or another. My worst conflicts to date were triggered just a few years ago when I became so obsessed with my lack of wealth, that I both struggled with and chased after wealth for a while. You will probably recognize yourself in some of these as well.

Chasers – Chasers have become overly fixated on chasing wealth. They seem to always be thinking about, conniving over, and chasing after various money-making schemes. Their single-mindedness, although sometimes appearing successful to the casual observer, rarely brings them lasting satisfaction. Regardless of what they are able to achieve financially, there's always more to be had. Therefore, their target for wealth is an ever-advancing one that's always ahead of them to chase. And chase they do!

Chasing wealth reflects a conflict with wealth because it's all-consuming. Wealth doesn't get directed into serving a greater good. Opportunities to fully experience life aren't seized upon because too many areas in life are being undervalued (such as health, relationships, family, community, creative expression, ethics, and higher aspirations).

Misers – Misers hold onto their wealth with a miserly tenaciousness. Even when they do acquire a fair amount of material wealth, consciously, they are still impoverished. Their lives continue to reflect an impoverished state. Due to their deep-seated fears of losing wealth again, they hoard it instead. They live as though they don't have wealth at all. Wealth fails to serve them in fully experiencing their lives because it isn't allowed to.

Misers live with a poverty consciousness. The tight grip they hold over their financial resources reflects a conflict with wealth because it doesn't allow a healthy flow (give and take) of wealth. Their wealth is almost exclusively allocated to survival, savings, and stockpiling. It's not uncommon for misers (and their dependents) to live in impoverished conditions, even when they have an abundance of financial resources available to them.

Projectors – Projectors desperately want to appear wealthy. They want to be recognized as being members of upper-crust societies. Of course, there's nothing wrong with wanting to be more successful than you are. In fact, stepping into a better role and telling a better story about your life are both keys to success. The conflict arises when projectors don't take the effective steps or extend the appropriate efforts to securely acquire what they are already projecting. It's not uncommon for projectors to take on enormous amounts of debt in their efforts to keep up appearances, which in turn makes it harder for them to establish real wealth.

Projecting wealth reflects a conflict with wealth because too much effort is spent on projecting illusionary wealth, and not enough on establishing real wealth. Wealth can't serve any greater purpose because it's not really there.

Strugglers – Strugglers always seem to be struggling with their ability to have and to hold onto enough resources to

159

make ends meet. To some degree, their struggle may be perpetuated by the fact that (at some point) they were living at the lower end of the socioeconomic spectrum, which means their odds for establishing wealth are legitimately stacked against them. Quite often, they must exercise more discipline to build material wealth than, let's say, someone who already has some financial reserves available to fall back on. That said, if someone is struggling with wealth from cradle to crypt, then it's less likely a life sentence and more likely a worthiness issue, or even a poverty consciousness that they are struggling with. Because of their difficult history, strugglers often have difficulty believing that they can do better in life. Unfortunately, that's a limiting belief, and it's limiting their ability to make plans and take actions that could substantially improve their financial reality.

Constantly struggling with wealth reflects a conflict with wealth that is rooted in a limiting belief system. Past difficulties or low self-esteem could be contributing to a jaded belief that lasting wealth is unattainable. People living with this conflict often give up on hopes and dreams that were, in actuality, achievable.

Objectors – Objectors resent wealth and everyone associated with it. Sometimes they are strugglers who feel like they are always on the outside looking in, which makes it easy for them to fall into resentment. Other times, objectors may be people who have witnessed or experienced too much abuse, exploitation, or gluttony from others experiencing their own conflicts with material wealth. People who object to wealth (and that can include the appearance of wealth) will often simultaneously desire, object to, and sabotage opportunities for greater wealth that come their way.

Objection to wealth reflects a conflict with wealth because preexisting prejudices sabotage present opportunities for wealth. People who object to wealth rarely fully experience life, because they are blocking a means (either consciously or subconsciously) for doing so.

Conflicts with wealth, like those listed above, are commonplace and oh so easy to fall into. Unfortunately, they all reflect an unhealthy relationship with material wealth. They demonstrate that far too many of us are far too focused on wealth itself, and not on the true and proper spirit that should exist behind wealth.

If you aren't using your wealth as a tool to fully experience your life, and if your wealth isn't serving you in serving some greater good in your life, then you are missing out on the point of wealth. You are probably living in some form of conflict with your material wealth.

Setting Things Right Again

On the flip side of that, once you can set things right again in your own mind, and shift your thinking so that your higher aspirations in life remain your primary focus; and once you remember that your wealth is meant to be a means for something else, and not just a means unto itself; then you can begin to realign your relationship with wealth back into its true and proper place. Once you can do that, your relationship with wealth should become easier, and you'll be able to get on track with your greater purpose in life.

Your conflicts with wealth will start remedying themselves once you remember that wealth is there to serve you in serving some greater good.

Dottie's Story

When I first moved to Sedona, I developed an instant friendship with the neighbor who lived behind me. Her name was Dottie. She was eighty-five years old at the time, and we shared a back fence. Dottie was this independent, spunky lady who seemed to know everyone and was at least a little bit involved in everything that went on in our little town.

Every day, it seemed, Dottie was out and about on an important mission. Some days, she helped out at her church. Other days, she volunteered at the Sedona Humane Society Thrift Store. Other days, she would be out shopping, visiting, or going to a special event. And on still other days, she might be getting her hair and nails done at the Classic Curls Salon. (Dottie's hair and nails were always in tip-top condition.)

Dottie had an interesting life story as well. She used to like to talk about what her life was like growing up on a farm in Iowa in the 1920s. She prided herself on the fact that she was good with horses, and that even as a very young girl, she would ride a horse out into the fields to bring water to the farmhands.

Life may have been generally good to Dottie, but it did not spare her from heartbreaks and traumas. Dottie's husband left her for another woman, leaving her heartbroken and alone to raise two young girls at a time when society was prone to look down on divorced women. The hurt of his betrayal never left her. Then there was the night the unthinkable happened. Her daughter, Kay, was killed in an automobile accident. Dottie would sometimes call me late at night because she saw my light on (and we were both night owls), and she would tearfully talk about Kay and how much she missed her. It was during one of those late-night chats that I learned the large plum tree in her back yard had been planted in memory of Kay.

Dottie wasn't a materially wealthy woman by any means. In fact, money was tight for her at times. Still, she had her devoted friends, and her other daughter, Pam (who was constantly checking in with her). She had her volunteer activities. She had a roof over her head. She had her older-model (yet immaculately maintained) bronze Cadillac, which meant she had her mobility and independence. Dottie lived a clean, simple life. She was blessed in that she remained clearheaded and in fairly good health her entire life. It wasn't unusual for me to glance out my living room window in the midafternoon and see her car driving by. There she'd go, sporting her dark wraparound sunglasses. Her hands would be gripped firmly on the steering wheel of her car as she concentrated on the road ahead of her. She was out and about and on her way to do something important!

Living and working in the town of Sedona, I got to know a lot of local folks. Many of them would be considered wealthy by anyone's definition! That said, very few fully experienced their lives to the degree that Dottie did. She had her essential needs taken care of and, therefore, she was free to live her life in a manner that was true to herself. Dottie was one of those special individuals who demonstrate their passion, purpose, and relevance in the world every day.

Dottie passed away at the respectable age of ninety-four. I know her final months were hard on her because she had to spend them in a hospice facility, and she didn't like that. But even when she was there at that facility, she never stopped being Dottie. Even as her body was failing her, she would sit and listen to someone else's problems. Even though she was barely able to cope herself, she was able to provide comfort and support to a dear and longtime friend of hers who was living out her final days at the same facility.

I will never forget Dottie, or the example she set by living her life as positively as she could, each and every day. Her priorities were always in the right place. As such, she always found the means to do what she felt compelled to do, which was usually to serve others in some way. Dottie was, without a doubt, one of those stellar examples of a human being who fully experienced life, regardless of the hand life dealt her.

Beacons

Little did I know that within a few years of moving to Sedona, my own health and finances would take a turn for the worse, and the ease I was accustomed to living my life with would slip away rather suddenly. That's when other positive souls out there, from various walks of life, stepped in and served as beacons, leading me back to positive thinking and living again.

Dottie was certainly one of those beacons. Regardless of the hardships and disappointments she endured over the years, she always found her way back to positive living. Her life never failed to reflect who she genuinely was or what her true values were.

Whereas, in comparison, my own sense of self evaporated once hardship hit. That's because my wealth really wasn't rooted in its true and proper place in my life. Outside of relocating to Sedona, I hadn't done anything with my wealth to personally grow or expand in any way. I certainly wasn't serving my community, or anyone else for that matter. I wasn't answering any higher calling either. If anything, I was hoarding my resources. My concept of wealth, it turned out, had been rather shallow and fear-based. As such, it was limiting my ability to fully experience my life.

In that sense, you could say that my financial downfall turned out to be a blessing in disguise. It brought about a sink-or-swim situation that ended up setting me right again. Once my focus got redirected back onto the positive things I wanted to accomplish and contribute to in my lifetime, regardless of my financial situation, then I was able to start fully experiencing my life again (where I was, as I was, with the resources I had). That shift in consciousness strengthened my sense of self and eventually my confidence, which in turn made it easier for me to succeed at future endeavors—including the financial ones!

Holistic Wealth: It's a Trinity

True wealth is so much more than the dictionaries depict. True wealth, when it sits in its true and proper spirit, is holistic in nature. It reflects a well-roundedness in life. True wealth, I believe, has three aspects of wellness to it:

Financial Wellness – Being able to adequately provide for yourself and your loved ones.

Physical Wellness – Having adequate health, mobility, and energy to do the things you want to do.

Spiritual Wellness – Living your life in such a way that your true values are expressed and you're serving some greater good.

This trinity of wellness not only enables you to live a life that functions, but it also ushers more authenticity and purpose into your life.

And here's the thing…

Personally, once I was able to wrap my brain around the idea that my wealth was meant to be a means for something else, and once I began using what resources I had to do the things my spirit was calling on me to do, then wealth realigned into its true and proper spirit in my life and my ability to generate wealth became easier! Of course, I still worried about money from time to time. I still had to apply strategies and wisdom to managing my finances. But I wasn't pining for or chasing after wealth anymore. I wasn't hoarding it so much eithcr. I was using what wealth I had to expand in ways that fostered a greater sense of purpose in my life.

That shift in thinking changed the way I made decisions and spent resources. It also marked a point in my life when I stopped floundering so much and began living with more intention.

Once you can approach your wealth holistically, and recognize that financial, physical, and spiritual wellness are all aspects of true wealth, then you can use your wealth to create a truly authentic and purposeful life. That's when wealth sits in its true and proper spirit.

Self-Worth

When you are *starting over* again in life, if you want to be genuinely happy and fulfilled this time around, you should probably try your best to manage your wealth holistically. You won't need to establish huge caches of material wealth, but you will need to be able to financially sustain yourself—practically and soundly. You will also need to be able to sustain your physical health and energy levels (to the best of your ability). And, perhaps most importantly, you will need to be able to direct some time and attention to things that allow your higher self to serve this world in a manner that expresses who you truly are.

Your willingness to be true to yourself and stay focused on your higher callings in life is how you're going to fundamentally reinforce your sense of self-worth. It's also how you're going to resolve any conflicts you might be having with your wealth, so that wealth can then flow more easily in your life.

"When you understand that your self-worth is not determined by your net worth, then you'll have financial freedom."
—Suze Orman

You *Can* Take It with You

There's an old adage that says, *"You can't take it with you."* It's often thrown out in connection with material wealth. It's certainly true enough when we're talking about material wealth alone. Let's face it, misfortune, aging, illness, dying, and death are the great equalizers in this world.

But I believe there is something you can develop in this lifetime that you can take with you when you pass out of this material world, and that's your consciousness. Your consciousness is an awareness (on some level) of how well you've experienced your life. It's an awareness of how you responded to the events that came your way. It's an awareness of how you treated people, and how you affected their lives. It's an awareness of the love you honored and allowed to exist, grow, and flourish in your lifetime. It's also an awareness of how you chose to express yourself and serve some greater good. I believe that these things come together to become part of a continuing consciousness. When some deeper part of you knows that you did your best to fully experience your life and accomplish something you came into this world to do, then surely that sense of accomplishment is something you take with you into the next grand adventure.

The sense of peace and satisfaction you get from fully experiencing your life and serving some greater good is something that becomes a part of you. It paints your soul in such a way—it can't be stripped away.

And that, my friends, has got to be the truest measure of wealth!

Practicalities

Chapter Ten

You have probably heard of the Law of Attraction. If you haven't, it goes something like this:

Stay focused on what you want in life (versus what you don't); envision your most positive future and sustain that vision; feel the essence of what you want as though it has already occurred; step into the role of who you want to be, even if you haven't fully manifested it yet; strive to tell the most positive story about yourself and your life; expect success; and then, if you can sustain these states of being well enough, for long enough, what you desire will be drawn to you.

Or, in other words…

Like attracts like. What you focus your attention and feelings on, good or bad, you will attract to you.

Obviously, I agree with most of that. In fact, many of the concepts discussed in this book blend beautifully with the Law of Attraction. That said, if I'm being perfectly honest, based on my experiences and observations, the Law of Attraction (in and of itself) isn't enough. I believe it's missing some major components needed for sustainable success.

Successful People

The most successful people I know—that is, the substantially successful people—do live their lives according to the basic principles behind the Law of Attraction. There's no question in my mind about that. They either do so consciously or subconsciously. But it's also been my observation that successful people are adept at something else—something that, according to some Law of Attraction practitioners, isn't even necessary. I beg to differ.

Highly functioning, successful people not only have an ability to attract opportunities, but they can identify, seize upon, build upon, and sustain those opportunities in ways that ensure lasting success.

They do this by blending their positive, can-do energy with something else—something I've come to refer to as the *practice of practicalities*.

Practicalities

Practicalities are those common-sense teachings we've been hearing about our entire lives. They are the wise life lessons our parents tried to instill in us, and our teachers tried to reinforce. They are the items employers like to tick off during performance reviews. They are the sentimentalities behind some of our most common clichés, such as *"A penny saved is a penny earned"* and *"You can lead a horse to water, but you can't make it drink."*

Practicalities are so ingrained in our social consciousness that a great many of you reading this chapter right now might be tempted to skip right over it—either because you believe you already know this stuff inside and out, and consider yourself more than adept at the practicalities of life, or because practicalities just aren't your thing. Maybe they're too rigid or mundane for you. Maybe you're more of the creative type and, as such, you aspire to live beyond the pragmatic pale, so to speak.

Whatever side of the fence you fall on when it comes to the *practice of practicalities*, I encourage you to read through this chapter anyway. Because when you are *starting over*, your world is turned upside down to a degree. Everything you think you know will be tested, at least a little. Your confidence will be challenged. Expect to go through some periods of discouragement and doubt as you continue on your *starting over* journey because it's inevitable. That said, *starting over* also prompts you to have greater aspirations for what you want your life to look like once you do get established again. These aspirations aren't mere fancies. They're being generated by something inside of you that's longing to be expressed. Therefore, when the inevitable conflict between aspiring for more, and pessimism over actually achieving it starts to play out in your mind, try to remember that, if utilized properly…

Practicalities will lend you reassurance during times of doubt because they are the solid stuff (the brick and mortar) that support your life. Practicalities will serve and support your creative visions as well.

So, even though this chapter may seem a little old-fashioned to some, and redundant to others, I encourage everyone to read through it anyway.

Good old-fashioned wisdom is still wisdom, after all, and redundancy is reaffirming!

Practical Adherence vs. Creative Expression

People who have come through particularly challenging times are especially proud of their practicalities. They are the folks who have struggled, skimped, saved, and adhered to the *practice of practicalities* well enough to establish well-functioning lives. Practically minded people derive a great deal of pleasure from having created something solid and sure for themselves and their loved ones. And rightfully so!

Things achieved through common-sense practicalities are (more often than not) substantial in nature. It takes dedication, focus, strategy, labor, organization, skill, endurance, and sometimes blood, sweat, and tears to create a well-functioning, practical life.

On the other hand, folks who are more idealistic and creative in nature (and I tend to fall into this category), as well as those who have observed the strictly practical as having incomplete lives (mostly in the areas of authenticity and creative expression), sometimes find themselves cringing at the very concept of "practical."

People who crave creative expression (like artists, writers, musicians, performers, entertainers, etc.), as well as those seeking to accomplish something extraordinary (like explorers, inventors, entrepreneurs, activists, etc.), often find the practice of practicalities constricting, when all they really want to do is expand.

Greater Practicalities

Both approaches to life are right, of course. And both, when they stand alone and discard the other, block out something important in life.

Creative expression and experimentation with little regard for life's more pragmatic side rarely achieve lasting success. Whereas pragmatic adherence without creative expression and experimentation rarely achieves personal fulfillment.

And that is as it should be. Because when you really stop to think about it, if you are seeking to fully experience life (as Henry David Thoreau so beautifully describes wealth), then *greater practicalities* need to be employed.

Greater practicalities incorporate practicalities that are both left- and right-brain inclusive, and are, therefore, more holistic in nature.

When you engage your *greater practicalities*, you are still able to adhere to the more common-sense practicalities to sustain a well-functioning life, but you can also engage in more creative and expansive thinking. This versatility will aid you greatly in areas like problem-solving, presentation, expression, and personal growth and development.

Both the creative and pragmatic approaches to life are practical when it comes to fulfilling their specific roles in your life. Greater practicalities integrate both approaches to help you realize your best possible life.

And really, when you stop to think about it, nothing is more practical than the desire to live your best possible life!

Marketing & Development: An Exercise in Greater Practicalities

Back in the nineties, I worked as a marketing and development officer for an environmental nonprofit organization in Washington, DC. I only worked there for a few years, but boy did that job prove to be pivotal to my personal development! In order to do it well, I had to learn how to combine my inherently creative nature with the more pragmatic skills of business. In other words, I had to employ my *greater practicalities* to reach my professional goals.

You see, every January, our CEO would meet with her VPs to relay the organization's goals and objectives for the upcoming year, as they were passed down to her by the board of directors. That meant that every January, the VPs would gather their teams together to pass down those same goals and objectives to them. And that meant that every January, the marketing and development team (all four of us) would gather in our VP's office to learn what our specific goals and objectives would be for the upcoming year. And that meant that every January, we walked into our VP's office to find some lofty and seemingly unattainable numbers scribbled out on a whiteboard. Those numbers were always higher and more daunting than they had been the year before. And that meant that every January, the marketing and development team would stand just inside our VP's office, a little gobsmacked as we stared at what seemed like our impossible financial goals for the upcoming year.

Yet as intimidating as those numbers may have been in January, by the time December rolled around (at least in the years I worked there), we had always reached them. That's because we quickly (and sometimes with a great deal of intention) shifted out of our collective pessimism and into a greater optimism instead. We got down to the business of figuring out how we were going to accomplish those goals.

That's when the magic started. That's when the whiteboards were cleared and multiple flip charts were erected. That's when the brainstorming began. That's when (quite literally) everything we could think of to raise money for the organization was thrown up on those boards to see what stuck.

No matter how weird an idea seemed at first blush, it was at least considered. It was put up on the board and given a hard look at. We couldn't afford to just offhandedly dismiss someone's creative idea, because we couldn't afford to shut down the creative flow of the group. If an idea passed some initial scrutiny, then it went into research. If it continued to hold up and remain a good, feasible idea for raising money, then it was mapped out into a plan, with objectives, steps, costs, timelines, and a budget, and that plan was acted upon and adhered to.

We may not have known it at the time, but we were actually taking our brainstorming sessions through the three required actions for *active hope* (*consideration*, *planning*, and *action*) to manifest our financial goals.

When all was said and done, it was the blending of our creative thinking, experimentation, and flexibility (all right-brain activities) with researching, planning, and budgeting (all left-brain activities) that engaged our *greater practicalities* and completed the skillset we needed to succeed. This holistic approach to fundraising was how we reached our ambitious financial goals for the organization, year after year after year.

The field of marketing and development is like one big exercise in greater practicalities. It's the perfect arena for blend-

ing creative idealism and problem-solving with pragmatic re-search, planning, and budgeting to achieve ambitious goals.

Making It Personal

When my life was seemingly falling apart a few years back, I had to find a way to pick up the pieces and start over again. I honestly didn't think I could do it at first. I wasn't in an optimistic frame of mind, that's for sure. My first big shift came when I got so disgusted with my life that I was able to shift out of my despair and into anger instead, and then into defiance. I had my *"So FN what!"* moment. My second big shift came when I reflected back on my days in marketing and development, and began applying some of the same approaches I had used in business to my personal life. In other words, I engaged my *greater practicalities.*

That's when the magic began to unfold in my personal life as well. That's when my hope rekindled. That's when I began brainstorming, researching, experimenting, planning, and acting on those plans to sort out my own life again.

I gave myself permission to experiment a little and go through a *period of discovery.* I pushed through my *resistance* and engaged my *sensitivities* in order to identify the people, places, and situations that resonated with me. Once I got into the flow (or *grace*) of aligning my life with situations that were a better fit for me, I experienced more success. The more success I experienced, the more confident I grew. The more confident I grew, the more positive I was about my future, because I knew I had recovered my skillset for success.

Let's face it, starting over in life and making a good go of it isn't impossible; it's always possible in some way, shape, or

176

form. But you must have the hope and confidence to aspire to it, and the greater practicalities to pull it off.

The Six Practicalities for Success

I believe there are six practicalities, in particular, that are vital for success in life. Combined, these practicalities can manifest just about any hopeful idea into reality.

The six practicalities for success include: the practicality of leadership; the practicality of living plans; the practicality of understanding your money; the practicality of presentation; the practicality of critical thinking; and the practicality of networking.

Below, I've gone over each of these practicalities in detail. Although these practicalities come out of the field of marketing and development, I've tweaked them a bit to make them more applicable to everyday life. Some of these practicalities will lean more towards pragmatism, while others will lean towards creative thinking. All will incorporate both left- and right-brain functionality to a degree, which is what also makes them *greater practicalities*.

These practicalities also contain exercises that have been designed to help you gain a clearer understanding and *feel* for how they work, as well as how to apply them to your everyday life. Whether you consider yourself left- or right-brain oriented, you will probably find yourself becoming resistant (at least a little) to doing some (if not all) of these exercises! Not because they're hard to do. They're not! They're remarkably easy to do. But because they all contain both pragmatic and creative aspects to them, which should make them equally repellant to everyone! That said, if you can commit to at least trying them, if only for a brief period of time, then I believe you're going to find yourself becoming more fluent at applying both ways of functioning to your everyday life. This will greatly serve you as you move forward to create a more holistic and satisfying life experience for yourself.

The Practicality of Leadership

The practicality of leadership dictates that you step into a leadership role in your own life. It's a commitment to living your life with more intention.

When you step into a leadership role in your own life, you take one hundred percent responsibility for your life—both the good and bad parts of it. You stop making excuses and deferring blame. You understand that by shucking your personal responsibility and shifting blame onto others, you give others too much power over your happiness and well-being. However, when you step into a leadership role in your life, you take back your personal power and start figuring things out again. You start intentionally and fully experiencing your life again. That's real power!

An Exercise in the Practicality of Leadership

My Life, Inc.

Imagine, if you will, that your life is a company: My Life, Inc. You are the new CEO hired to come in and steer this company in a new and better direction. Starting where you are, with the resources you already have, see yourself taking those reins. Start strategizing like a CEO. Identify your mission statement (that is, what do you want your life to represent?). Try entertaining some new and creative ideas. Think outside the box. Set some new goals for yourself. Start making decisions and taking actions that you think will take My Life, Inc. in a better direction.

To help you really get into the *feel* of your new executive role, try conducting an imaginary staff meeting!

When you are alone, and no one is around to judge or ridicule you, call a pretend staff meeting. Stand at the front of a room and try to imagine your staff sitting dutifully before you, awaiting your instructions. Take a pretend roll call. Speak out loud. Identify a pretend Chief Financial Officer, a pretend Chief Operations Officer, a pretend Chief Creative Officer, and whoever else you think you need on your team. Give them pretend names. Tell them about your objectives and goals for the company. Ask for their input. Pretend they are answering you and giving you helpful suggestions. What did they say? Jot it down. Take notes. Heck, erect some flip charts if that helps you get into the *feel* of your new executive role!

Remember when you were a child and you pretended things all the time? Well, you may have been pretending, but you were also role-playing and developing important life skills. Holding an imaginary staff meeting is a playful game on the one hand (anyone can do it), while on the other hand, you are exercising the important skill of leadership. As you act out your imaginary staff meeting, you are getting familiar with stepping into your leadership role. You are engaging your executive mind without taking on any real risks (other than perhaps feeling a bit foolish). Your creative mind is engaged, and at the same time you are problem-solving and coming up with some viable ideas.

You don't want to be a mere employee, officer, manager, or even VP in your own life. Because when all is said and done, only you are held accountable for how you lived your life. Therefore, step into your power. Assume your full leadership role. Become the Principal, the CEO of your own life!

Now is not the time to be wishy-washy about your leadership skills. You are the only person on this planet qualified enough to know what's truly right for you. Engage your *greater practicalities*. Be strategic and pragmatic on the one hand, and creative and expansive on the other. You want to get accustomed to both taking and managing risks. A good leader assigns value to every department in his or her company, including legal, accounting, budgeting, research, outreach, marketing, sales, project development, engineering, personnel, customer service, technology, etc. Some departments lean more towards pragmaticism, while others are more creative in nature. Yet if any one department is underutilized, the entire company suffers.

The Practicality of Living Plans

The practicality of living plans dictates that anything that is possible, no matter how difficult, can be achieved with the right plan.

One of the great predictors of success in our world is the presence of a well-crafted plan. A good plan is a powerful tool for success.

That said, even good plans can become limiting in certain situations. Therefore, the best-made plans incorporate the *greater practicalities* by being more flexible and subjective. I like to refer to them as *living plans* because, as you continue to work with them, they adjust and change as circumstances adjust and change.

Living plans work like all living documents: they are writ-ten, directive, and adhered to. But they are also revisited and revised as circumstances, desires, and goals change.

An Exercise in The Practicality of Living Plans

Constructing a Plan

Stepping into your role of CEO of My Life, Inc., try drafting a plan for something you've always wanted to do. This is just an exercise, so choose something that's fun and easy to accom-plish, like taking a day trip somewhere. Whatever you choose, plan it out well in advance and follow through with it.

Keep in mind that all good plans have key components to them. They should...

- Have a mission statement.
- Be in writing.
- Define goals.
- List step-by-step actions.
- Allot time and resources for research and develop-ment.
- Set time frames.
- Include costs and a budget.
- Identify financial resources.

And, since your plan will also be a living plan, it should...

- Be revisited and adjusted as shifting circumstances and desires require.

If a good plan is a powerful tool for success, then a good living plan is a superpower.

While being too loosey-goosey with your plans can be the kiss of death for them, so can being too rigid. If your plans aren't organic enough to adjust to real-life changes (and even some exceptions), then, at some point, they're probably going to fail you.

The Practicality of Understanding Your Money

The practicality of understanding your money dictates that you stay on top of your financial reality. It includes an understanding that only you can ultimately decide how best to save, invest, and spend your financial resources so that you are both secure and fulfilled in life.

If you have stepped into a leadership role in your life, then you don't want to become complacent in the area of your finances. Nor do you want to just arbitrarily hand over that responsibility to someone else. Of course, you should be open to soliciting and weighing advice from others who are more experienced in the field of money management. And, you should be open to learning everything you can about effectively managing your own money so that you are equipped to make good financial decisions for yourself. But you shouldn't just hand off your financial responsibilities to another. You shouldn't neglect your finances in any way either. Quite literally, your buck stops with you.

Giving up control of your finances doesn't pair well with the practicality of leadership. Understanding your money does.

Let's return to the role of a CEO. A good CEO commits to understanding the ins and outs of all the areas in his or her company. A good CEO will consult with different department heads and advisors for insight and guidance. But a good CEO will always make the final decisions. Why? Because the responsibility for how those decisions pan out will ultimately fall back on the CEO. The same holds true for you in your life and with your money.

Only you can truly know what elements you need to have in place to fully experience your life.

Some folks will need large caches of financial reserves tucked away in order to feel secure and relieve their anxieties about the future. Others might need to raise a huge sum of capital to fund something they've always been impassioned to do. Still others might require only modest amounts of income and reserves and still be able to live out their lives in a full and meaningful way. The idea that we all need tons of money tucked away in order to have a good future is a myth. We're all different, and we have different financial needs and objectives.

By the truest measure of your wealth, you need enough money to fully experience your life, and to continue fully experiencing your life, whatever that means to you.

The good news is that…

The better you understand your money, the better your financial decisions will be.

I'm not a money manager. I don't know your unique financial requirements. Therefore, I can't, with a clear conscience, offer you specific money management strategies. But I can say confidently that almost anyone can learn to manage their money better once they understand their money better. In fact, most of the financial mistakes I see people making (including many of my own) have come from a lack of understanding about what their financial situation really is and how their money is working (or not working) for them. Or, in other words…

Better money management begins with understanding your money better, and then by doing the math.

An Exercise in Understanding Your Money

The Money Diary

One of the most effective tools I've discovered for better understanding my money is something called a *money diary*. I was turned onto this technique a few years ago by a customer visiting an art gallery I worked at. I've been using it and recommending it to others ever since.

In this exercise, you'll want to get a brand-new notebook to designate as your money diary.

Your money diary is a journal that documents and tracks your entire financial reality.

I recommend keeping your money diary active and current through at least one billing cycle (that's thirty days), if not longer, if not indefinitely!

Divide your money diary into two sections. *Section one* will be for documenting your *financial profile,* and *section two* will be for keeping a running total of your available *cash flow.*

Personally, I like to dedicate the left-hand pages of my money diary to my financial profile, and the right-hand pages for the running total of my cash flow. That way, I can reconcile the information on both sides of the diary every time I turn the page and I have a snapshot of my entire financial reality at my fingertips at any given point in time.

When starting your own money diary, don't worry so much about acting on the information you're discovering. Just discover it for now. Know your financial truth—both the good and the bad aspects of it. Your instincts and personal value system will eventually come forward and prompt you to make certain changes in your finances. But for now, don't focus on that. For now, the purpose of your money diary is to gain knowledge.

Constructs of a Money Diary – Section One: Financial Profile

This is where you want to research and document your financial profile, which includes the following information:

Triple Borough Credit Scores – Note your scores, factors affecting your scores, and anything else you can think of that might improve your credit.

Financial Accounts – List all banking, investment, and money market accounts. Include institution names, account numbers, balances, fees, penalties, and interest rates.

Revolving Lines of Credit – List all creditors. Include creditor names, account numbers, balances, fees, penalties, and interest rates.

Loans – List all personal, student, vehicle, mortgage, and business loans. Include lender names, account numbers, balances, fees, penalties, and interest rates.

Sources of Income – Include all sources of income from employment, businesses, investments, and rents, as well as informal sources of income. Prorate all income to monthly (if you estimate, estimate low).

Monthly Expenses – Research and list all anticipated monthly expenses. Make sure to include groceries, fuel, utilities, rents, mortgages, bills, taxes, memberships, subscriptions, insurances, etc. Prorate all expenses to monthly (if you estimate, estimate high).

Potential Sources for Additional Capital – Brainstorm and try to identify any potential sources for additional money that you might be able to tap into in a pinch. These sources might include personal loans, grants, increasing existing credit lines, withdrawing funds, liquidating assets, or taking on supplemental employment.

Miscellaneous – Leave room to document anything else that you think might be relevant to your financial profile.

Constructs of a Money Diary – Section Two: Cash Flow

This is where you want to combine all your available cash flow sources (including cash, checking, debit, and money market activity), and keep a running tally of your available cash in a ledger-like format, just as you would when balancing a checkbook.

Incoming Cash Flow – Track and add up all income, deposits, and monetary gifts contributing to your available cash flow.

Outgoing Cash Flow – Track and subtract all spending in the form of cash, checks, debits, withdrawals, and automated payments from your available cash flow total.

Once you get your money diary up and running, you're going to immediately have a better understanding of your financial reality. You'll gain a greater sense of control over your finances as well. With time, you should rather effortlessly progress into coming up with ways to make your money work better for you.

Whether you consider yourself good at money management, or not so good, this exercise can only improve your financial reality. How do I know that? Well, first, because knowledge is your first step towards mastery. And second, because...

Like attracts like. By creating and maintaining a money diary, you are directing time, attention, and energy into your financial reality, which, given time, will attract a better financial reality to you!

(IMPORTANT NOTE: All diaries are deeply personal accountings. Your money diary is no exception. Never leave it lying around where prying eyes with dishonorable intent can discover it. If you can, keep it under lock and key.)

The Practicality of Presentation

The practicality of presentation dictates that you give care and attention to your physical and environmental presentation, so that these things continue to reflect who you are and how you want to be perceived by the world.

This practicality is used all the time in marketing. It aligns rather beautifully with the principles behind the Law of Attraction because it reinforces the energetic template for how you want to be perceived by the world. It consciously and subconsciously affects the way you perceive yourself, as well as how others perceive you, and, subsequently, the degree of respect and opportunities that others are willing to extend to you.

You never want to underestimate the power of your personal presentation because it's always affecting your life, whether you're aware of it or not.

Some people really drop the ball when it comes to their personal presentation—I think, perhaps, because they think it's pretentious on some level. But the *practicality of presentation* isn't asking you to pretend. In fact, it's asking you to do the opposite. It's asking you to identify who you are, authentically, and then reflect your authenticity in every aspect of your life. Once you understand that your presentation is a means for expressing (and reaffirming) your truth, then I think you'll see that it's really your lack of presentation that's portraying falsity, because it reflects nothing at all about you. You are not nothing! You are something!

Your authentic self is your truth. Your truth has a unique energy and contribution to make. How you present yourself to the world will either attract or deter things that align with your truth.

Returning to the narrative of the CEO of My Life, Inc.: nothing devalues a company faster than the loss of identity, and without a consistent presentation, identity can falter.

An Exercise in the Practicality of Presentation

Create a Vision Board

Every day, for about a week or so, comb through magazines and online sources to look for images that resonate with you. They really can be anything that makes you feel good (like images of fishing, boating, colors, houses, clothing, cars, people, animals, flowers, gardening, working, landscapes, and places near and far). Basically, if it strikes a positive chord in you, then print or cut it out, and start collecting your images in a folder.

After you've collected a fair number of images, get a large sheet of posterboard and begin gluing your images onto it in a collage-like fashion. Be as artistic, creative, or messy as you want. This exercise is for your benefit and no one else's, so don't stress out if it's not going to win any design awards. Simply have fun with this exercise. When you're done, stand back and take a good, hard look at what you've just created. What mood does it convey? What principles (if any) are coming forward? What is the overall story and vibe you get when you look at your vision board?

Now, going forward, try to make this vision board a sort of template for how you present yourself to the world. You don't have to duplicate the images precisely, just try to replicate the vibe they collectively convey as you go about your life.

There's nothing pretentious about presenting yourself in a way that reflects who you really are, or who you aspire to be, or what truly resonates with you. Chances are, you've gotten rather complacent about your personal presentation to the world. So, at least for a while, you might feel somewhat conspicuous as you discover and get used to living in a more authentic energy. Certainly others will take notice, and this might cause you to feel uncomfortable for a while.

Eventually, you'll become so accustomed to expressing a better version of yourself that you won't want to return to that rather nondescript person you were settling for. That's when you will have advanced to a whole new level of existence. That's when a slew of new opportunities will start coming your way—opportunities more aligned with who you really are and aspire to be!

Your personal presentation is a part of your message to the world. Stay on track with your message so that you can attract more personally authentic things to you.

The Practicality of Critical Thinking

The practicality of critical thinking dictates that you understand how cause and effect are affecting your life, so that you might then go on to make better decisions based on that understanding.

There are countless studies, curriculums, books, puzzles, games, tips, and exercises out there for improving your critical thinking skills. Yet be that as it may, if you look around you today, I think you will agree that there is a gross deficiency in critical thinking being demonstrated in society at large. I suppose there are multiple reasons for this, such as nutritional deficiencies, illnesses, cognitive disorders, stress, distractions, limited information, manipulative information, and lazy thinking, to name a few. But there is one contributor that stands out to me. In fact, it's such a monkey wrench in the cogs of critical thinking that when it's skillfully applied, I swear, otherwise intelligent people just can't seem to add two plus two together! This great detractor just happens to be something that I'm familiar with because it comes out of the field of marketing. It's known as *branding*.

Branding is a consistent and repetitive presentation that seeks to define and then strengthen the identity of its subject.

When applied in sales, branding identifies and emphasizes the positive attributes of a product so that the public is aware of them. This helps to sell the product!

The Art of Branding

In sales, the most effective branding campaigns have at least four components to them: definition, recognition, emotional triggers, and repetition.

Definition – Clarify what the product is and does.

Recognition – Attach consistent and recognizable symbolism (such as logos, colors, jingles, catchphrases, etc.).

Emotional Triggers – Introduce elements that are meant to trigger an emotion (such as emotionally charged words, phrases, symbols, music, imagery, etc.).

Repetition – Present the now *branded* product to the public through a campaign of ongoing exposure.

When these four components are in place, the odds for a successful sales campaign go way up.

When consumers understand a product; recognize a product; experience positive emotions in relation to a product; and are then exposed to the (now branded) product over and over again, consumers start to desire the product.

That's how branding drives sales. That's also why you find so many feel-good images in advertising (such as active people enjoying healthy lifestyles, trendy home settings, smiling couples holding hands, and happy children playing with cute pets).

When the art of branding is successfully applied, it intro- duces a positive message about a product into the observer's subconscious. Eventually, an automatic positive response to the product is engaged, whereas a more critical response to that same product is disengaged.

Here's an example of how that works:

The Summer Outreach Campaign

When I was working in marketing and development, our organ- ization maintained something called the Contributors' Data- base. That database held the names and addresses of all our dues-paying members, as well as anyone who had made finan- cial contributions through donations, attending events, or pur- chasing products. We were constantly mailing out material to the people on that database. Every time we did a mailing, we made sure that the content prominently displayed our organiza- tion's name, logo, and a heartwarming blurb summarizing our mission statement. By doing so, we made sure that our mail- ings were properly branded.

One summer, we mailed out note cards to everyone on that database. These cards were white with simply sketched wild- flowers on the front. Inside the cards was an offer to purchase boxes of these same cards. We assured recipients that their purchase would go towards supporting our eco-restoration pro- jects, as well as help an aspiring new artist gain some well- deserved recognition. The database was then sorted according to two political affiliations: Conservative and Liberal. (Yes, we kept track of that kind of thing!) Both groups were mailed the same note cards with the same sketched flowers on the front, and the same solicitous message inside. However, the wording on the front of the cards was changed slightly to better appeal to its targeted group. Cards going to Conservatives began with

"Help Us Save Our Land," whereas cards going to Liberals began with *"Help Us Save the Earth."*

It was time-consuming and costly to do the multiple printings, but was it worth it? The short answer is: yes, it was! Because these two groups predictably respond to words differently. Conservatives have a more positive emotional response to the words *"our land,"* whereas Liberals have a more positive emotional response to the words *"the Earth."* That's not just a hypothesis; it's a fact as far as environmental marketing is concerned. If we screwed up and accidentally mailed out a batch with the wrong wording for its targeted group (which we occasionally did), then the response rate for that mailing (which we tracked) went down.

Although both groups could appreciate a healthy environment and artistic note cards, our favorable presentation to those groups could be either enhanced or hindered based on the wording we chose to use. That's how branding works and why it's such a powerful tool in sales.

Political Branding

Marketers use branding all the time to sell their products, but they aren't the only ones. Today, any entity seeking public support applies the *art of branding* in some way, shape, or form to harness that support. But none are more apt at doing so than political organizations.

Powerful political organizations, as well as their organizational supporters (including corporations, industries, nonprofits, religious organizations, and large special interest groups of all kinds), have become so skilled at the art of branding, they've raised it to a science!

Identity Factors

Political branding incorporates extremely powerful emotional triggers into the agendas they are trying to sell the public on. These triggers are known as *identity factors*. When successfully applied, identity factors become much more embedded in the public's subconscious than, let's say, a cute puppy, or an attractive person jogging in the park.

Identity factors are those things we hold near and dear because they reinforce our sense of identity. They can consist of things such as causes, interests, hobbies, fraternities, sororities, clubs, activities, socioeconomics, etc. But the most emotionally charged and, therefore, powerful identity factors are tribal. They consist of things such as race, gender, religion, nationality, and cultural similarities that reflect race, gender, religion, and nationality.

Negative Branding

Political branding also incorporates negative branding, which works the same way that all branding does, only through negativity. Political entities *define* their competition negatively by attaching negative *symbolism* to them. Then they introduce negative *emotional triggers* designed to stir up negative emotions. Then finally, they expose their now negatively branded opposition to the public through *repetitious* campaigning.

When political branding (both the positive and negative aspects of it) is successful, it links our sense of identity to an emotionally charged political agenda. Once a manufactured emotionally charged response to an agenda is engaged, critical thinking about that agenda is disengaged.

Cognitive Dissonance

So, why is political branding such a big deal, and how could it be contributing to the lack of critical thinking we're witnessing in the world today? Because it's so emotionally charged that it overrides the critical thought process in our brains. This can lead to dichotomous thought patterns, which in turn can lead to a mental state of cognitive dissonance.

Once cognitive dissonance is accepted by the brain, it can become a pattern in the brain. When that happens, cognitive dissonance can affect every aspect of a person's life, political or otherwise.

The more accustomed our brains become to accepting multiple presentations of conflicting information as true, the more disconnected we become from understanding how true cause and effect works in our world and, consequently, in our personal lives. Once we fail to recognize true cause and effect, we fail to make the best decisions for ourselves, our families, our businesses, and our communities.

"Political language is designed to make lies sound truthful and murder respectable and to give an appearance of solidarity to pure wind." —George Orwell

So, what can you (as an individual) do to sidestep the constant barrage of manipulative marketing campaigns, so that you can decipher information realistically and go on to make better decisions for yourself?

An Exercise in Critical Thinking

Cutting Ties that Brand

This exercise is designed to work in two parts: first, it seeks to disconnect you from the outside manipulation triggering your automatic emotional responses; and second, it seeks to intercept your automatic emotional responses.

I've been doing this exercise off and on for years now, and I've noticed a huge change in my overall judgement and decision-making skills—all for the better! My emotional, knee-jerk responses to everyday frustrations are more tempered. That's a far cry from my younger days when I could find myself devastated and immobilized by a life crisis. Today, I'm more level-headed and confident as a rule. Once I have the real facts at hand, I know that I can figure things out and handle just about anything life throws at me. That's a great mental space to be in!

Cutting Ties that Brand, Step One: Shutting Out the Noise

Shutting out the noise is an exercise that should be done for at least ten days, but it seems to work optimally for me when sustained for fifteen days. It involves a media fast, which includes all forms of social media, cable news, opinionated news, political documentaries, political books and magazines, and politically charged events. It can even include distancing yourself from certain friends and relatives (to the degree that you can) who frequently express political opinions.

You can still listen to your local news. Afterall, you don't want to be totally cut off from what's going on around you. But local news, for the most part, is apolitical. It tells you (rather clinically) what you need to know to stay informed as it quickly moves from subject to subject.

When the fifteen days are up and the exercise is complete, you're going to be ready to jump into the fray of everyday life again. As well you should be! But you're going to feel better and think more clearly when you do.

Shutting out the noise by distancing yourself from politically charged venues and opinions allows your brain a respite from political conditioning. By the end of this exercise, you should notice that you are thinking for yourself again and feeling better about life in general.

Shutting out the noise is an exercise you'll want to do from time to time—basically, any time you find yourself moving into extended states of stress, anger, or anxiety over the state of our world today. *Shutting out the noise* gives your brain a kind of vacation! Have you ever noticed how relaxed and centered you are after a good vacation? Well, this exercise gives your brain that same chance to reset.

Cutting Ties that Brand, Step Two: Meditation of Non-Judgement

I was turned on to the *meditation of non-judgement* by a yoga instructor. It's an active form of meditation, which means you're not going to be doing a meditation session. Instead, you're going to be living your life as you normally would, only with more mindfulness for a set period of time.

In the last three days of your media fast (so starting on day twelve if you're doing a fifteen-day media fast), you're not going to judge anyone based on preconceptions or stereotypes. In particular, you're not going to make a single judgement based on a person's race, gender (this includes gender identification), religion, nationality, age, socioeconomics, style, or appearance. And, you're not going to judge anyone based on their political affiliations either. When you notice a stereotypical judgement towards another person popping into your head, with your thoughts, repeat this mantra:

I release all judgement of you. I release all judgement of myself.

That's it. That's the second half of the exercise! But fair warning: it's harder to do than it seems.

We are constantly judging others. We can't pass a single person on the street without making a snap judgement about them. It's automatic. Therefore, this part of the exercise is going to be extremely difficult to maintain at first. On day one, you're probably going to be repeating your mantra of non-judgement constantly! That's okay. It gets easier on day two! And by day three, your tendency to automatically judge others based on anything other than how they are treating you in the moment will be greatly diminished. You'll notice that you are responding to people and events as they are, not as you're projecting them to be. That's a beautiful thing! That's the point of the exercise.

Look, critical thinking is a vital part of successful living. You need to be able to perceive and respond to your world realistically, so that you can go on to make the best decisions for yourself and remain standing in your personal power (versus serving someone else's agenda).

You don't want to waste your precious mental and emotional energy fighting phantoms or automatically reacting to contrived emotional triggers.

The Practicality of Networking

And last but not least, there is the *practicality of networking.*

The practicality of networking dictates that you allot the appropriate time, effort, and attention to your relationships, because you understand that successful living and successful relationships are inevitably linked.

You can be qualified, skilled, experienced, and hardworking. You can be credentialed. But if you fail to connect well with others, and sustain those connections, then you can still find yourself with the short end of the stick when it comes to securing some good opportunities out there. You can be immensely talented and downright brilliant, and yet still find yourself undermined when it comes to snagging that carrot you had your sights on. When that happens, it's usually because whoever held that carrot connected better with someone else. As unfair as that might feel at the time, it's also a reality of our world. You can either find yourself incessantly angry and resentful because of the unfairness of it all, or you can learn your lesson sooner rather than later and get to work improving your networking skills.

When you bring credentials, skill, and dedication to the table, and you are properly networked and connecting well with others, you launch your ambitions into a whole new ballpark of success.

Networking is connecting. It's extending time and energy to family, friends, neighbors, acquaintances, colleagues, and business associates in an effort to make new connections and strengthen existing relationships.

It's an Exchange of Energy

Let's say you have a desire to move into another line of work, or perhaps you want to go back to school, or start a business, or explore a creative endeavor... then I'm going to suggest that you start engaging with others in those same fields of interest. In general, consider joining more groups, clubs, or organizations that interest you.

Also, try getting accustomed to inviting people out for lunch. Dare to have a get-together at your home to get to know your neighbors better. Volunteer somewhere. Look for opportunities to help others in need. These things will tax your energy initially, yes, but they will also be an energetic investment.

Your network is an investment of personal energy that will eventually return to you multiplied—often when you need it the most.

Once you get into the flow of networking, you'll be amazed at the increased number of opportunities that come your way. You'll be surprised by the new pathways that simply open up before you.

Networking connects you with others through an exchange of energy. It allows you to serve and be served. It's going to be through your connections that you come to realize your purpose in life. It's going to be through networking that opportunities come your way.

An Exercise in Networking

The Tree Meditation

When you have a quiet block of time available, find a comfortable chair and sit down in it. Close your eyes and take some deep breaths. Once you feel relaxation settling in, with your eyes still closed, take a deep breath in through your nose and hold it to the count of three. Then release your breath slowly out through your mouth. Repeat this metered breathing for three cycles. Then, with your eyes still closed, slowly count backwards from ten to one.

Now, try to imagine that you are a tree. See yourself planted firmly in the earth in a vast and beautiful forest. Imagine sunlight filtering down through your outstretched canopy. Feel your leaves soaking in air and sunshine as you shimmer in a soft breeze. Envision the air and sunshine photosynthesizing inside of you, turning into chlorophyll and infusing your leaves with a rich green color. Feel the vascular system in your trunk drawing up sweet hydration and nutrients through your roots, then distributing this life-giving sustenance throughout your branches. You are a healthy, happy tree living in a healthy, happy forest and, as such, all your needs are plentifully met. You are slowly growing up and branching out in health.

Now, think about your root system for a moment. It needs to grow down and spread out. Because if it doesn't, you might topple over the next time a strong wind blows through the forest! Now, think of your relationships as your roots. Understand that with each sincere connection you make, you put down more roots. Each time you reach out to nurture your existing relationships, you nurture and grow your existing roots. See your roots growing deep, wide, and strong, to the extent that you are now a strong, secure tree that can withstand any storm. Once you have sustained this vision for a few minutes, you are ready to come out of your meditation. Slowly count from one to ten and open your eyes.

From this point on, as you go about your everyday life, try to seize upon opportunities to connect with others and grow your roots. Even if you're tired or busy, at least take some time to do simple things (like responding by calling or texting). When you have more time and energy available to you, consider visiting, serving, or giving someone a gift, because these ac-

201

tions will strengthen your roots. Keep in mind that some of your roots will run deep, while others will be shallower and more secondary in nature. Still others will run up against obstacles and fail to continue. It's all good! Keep putting down your roots. Keep strengthening the stability of your tree!

Keep nurturing your social network by putting down and nourishing your social roots! That way, when the ill winds of life blow (and they will blow), your chances for survival will be greatly enhanced because your root system will run deep and strong.

The Well-Rounded Approach

The main principle behind the Law of Attraction is indeed powerful: *Like attracts like.* There's no question about that. Once you're able to shift your thinking and behavior so that your energy is more aligned with the things you want in life, the Universe shifts with you and you start attracting better scenarios into your life. But you don't want to simply attract things. You want to be able to recognize and seize upon the opportunities that come your way. You want to be able to sustain them and then build upon them. That's where the *practice of practicalities* and, particularly, the *greater practicalities* come into play.

By stepping into your *leadership* role; and by effectively *planning* things out; and by *understanding your money*; and by putting effort into your personal *presentation* to the world; and by strengthening your *critical thinking* skills; and by being properly *networked*; you are going to be practically equipped for success in whatever you aspire to do.

Even Henry David Thoreau had to have his more commonplace practicalities in place to be able to live simply in

Walden Wood and write. He had to have permission from his good friend and mentor, Ralph Waldo Emerson, the landowner. He had to have prearranged provisions and sustenance to fall back on. Once his basic practicalities were in place, his *greater practicalities* were engaged, and he was free to dedicate his time and attention to writing volumes of poetry, essays, and prose, which have inspired so many of us down through the ages.

Once our greater practicalities are engaged, we can create a life that not only functions, but is also creative, expressive, and fulfilling. That's the well-rounded approach.

WRENS

Chapter Eleven

(IMPORTANT NOTE: The information provided below is not intended to be a substitute for professional medical advice or services. The information provided should not be used for diagnosing or treating a health problem or disease, and those seeking personal medical advice should consult with a licensed physician.)

Mornings in my garden are nothing less than enchanting when the sweet little wrens show up for their visit. Their songs are strong and sonorous and have a way of piercing through my preoccupations—even the troubling ones.

Little Ambassadors of Health

These tiny bundles of tireless energy always seem to be busy doing something. Here, in Arizona, it's not unusual to see both the males and females building multiple nests, each nestled protectively in the arms of cacti, like first, second, and third homes. Yet as busy as they always seem to be throughout their days, when the sun finally sets low in the sky, and then again when it rises, these industrious little creatures never fail to pause and offer up a song. They live simple lives of singing, toiling, singing, and resting, just to do it all again the next day. They are the perfect examples of all things bright and industrious, yet balanced in rest, enjoyment, and self-expression, which is why I have chosen them to be our little ambassadors of health.

The WRENS

And, just like the lives of little wrens, the components needed for you to maintain your body in a bright, industrious, and yet balanced state are also relatively simple.

There are basically five needs that must be met so that your body can maintain its natural balance. These five needs are adequate measures of water, rest, exercise, nutrition, and (when needed) support. Or, as the acronym so conveniently sums up, your body requires its WRENS.

When these five needs are met, your body is better balanced and better able to maintain its healthy state. It's also better able to recover from health issues that will inevitably show up.

By tending to your WRENS today, you can help ensure that the next chapter in your life's story will unfold to be the best it can be.

Neglecting Your WRENS

The problem is that most of us tend to neglect at least some of these basic needs as we go about our daily lives. We might have one or two of them in place, but we fail to integrate all of them, concurrently, no matter how simple or basic they may be. That's when we set ourselves up for health issues.

When your body fails to secure the basics it needs to sustain health, it falls out of its natural order. That's when disorder sets in, and, eventually... disease.

So, let's take a closer look at these five needs (or WRENS), and by doing so, hopefully get them better integrated into your daily routine.

What, specifically, are the WRENS, and how do they contribute to your overall health?

The WRENS – Water

Did you know that water makes up over two-thirds of a healthy human being's body? Your muscles are comprised of seventy-five percent water, your brain of eighty-five percent water, and your living cells of seventy percent or more of water. Therefore, it goes without much argument that...

Your body requires proper hydration in order to function optimally, right down to the cellular level.

"Water helps to restore fluids lost through metabolism, breathing, sweating, and the removal of waste. It helps to keep you from overheating, lubricates the joints and tissues, maintains healthy skin, and is necessary for proper digestion. It's the perfect zero-calorie beverage for quenching thirst and re-

hydrating your body."—Harvard School of Public Health[1]

Yet be that as it may, according to multiple studies, a whopping seventy-five percent of us probably suffer from some degree of chronic dehydration, which triggers a host of other illnesses. Sadly, these illnesses are almost never associated with dehydration in their early stages, when there is still a window of time open to prevent them.

"Over time, failure to drink enough water can contribute to a wide array of medical complications, from fatigue, joint pain and weight gain to headaches, ulcers, high blood pressure and kidney disease." —Panorama Now[2]

Some Friendly Advice

A few years ago, when I was checking into my rheumatologist's office for the first time, the receptionist at the front desk offered me a cup of water from the nearby water cooler. I thanked her, but declined her offer because I really wasn't thirsty at the time. Then, as the medical assistant was taking my vitals, she too offered me some water. Again, I thanked her, but declined. Then, once again, while in my first consultation with my new doctor, he too offered me water! At that point, I laughed and said something like "Wow, this office is sure into

---

[1] "Water," Harvard School of Public Health, https://www.hsph.harvard.edu/nutritionsource/water/.

[2] Sue Baxter, "How Drinking Water May Save Your Life!", Panorama Now, https://panoramanow.com/how-drinking-water-may-save-your-life/.

water!" To which my new doctor replied (quite seriously, I might add), "I can't stress enough the importance of proper hydration. Once I get my patients to increase their water intake, in many cases, their muscle stiffness and joint pain decrease. Sometimes significantly so." I was surprised to hear that.

Years later, as I was standing in my driveway, chatting with my next-door neighbor about some leg pain I was experiencing at night, he too brought up water. He went on to say that when he plays golf, if he doesn't drink enough water leading up to the game, he experiences terrible leg pain at night. I was skeptical that something as simple as drinking more water during the day could actually address my nightly leg pain, but I was willing to give it a shot. I started drinking more water during my days—significantly more. Within a few days of doing so, my nightly leg pain decreased—significantly so!

Aversion to Drinking Water

I have no doubt that many of us are walking around in a dehydrated state to some degree. And here's the thing: personally, once I become chronically dehydrated (as opposed to acutely dehydrated, like after a long, hot hike), I often don't crave water. I might want a soda, or a cup of coffee, or tea, or even a glass of juice. But I rarely crave a nice, tall glass of pure, clean water, even though that's exactly what my body needs at the time.

I doubt that I'm the only one who experiences an occasional aversion to drinking plain water. However, now that I'm aware of the signs of chronic dehydration (such as crepey skin, dry mouth, dark urine, puffy eyes, headaches, increased muscle and joint pain, and even water retention), and the positive health benefits of drinking more water, I push through my resistance and drink more water anyway. That's usually when something rather remarkable starts to happen about twenty-four to forty-eight hours later. I start craving water again, even over coffee, tea, soda, or juice. That's when I know my body is sorting itself out. That's also when I start feeling better, generally speaking.

Making Hydration Enjoyable!

If you are like me, and find yourself experiencing an occasional aversion to drinking plain water, there's no need to stress out about it! There are some simple things you can do to make your fluid intake more enjoyable, so that you can still go on to maintain proper hydration and subsequently your overall health. I've listed a few ideas below:

Lemon Water

Adding freshly squeezed lemon juice to your drinking water freshens it up nicely and adds a cool, citrusy taste. Additionally, according to LifeHack.org, there are at least eleven additional health benefits your body may receive from drinking lemon water:

Lemon water

- *Boosts your immune system.*
- *Is an excellent source of potassium.*
- *Aids in digestion.*
- *Cleanses your system (particularly the kidneys and liver).*
- *Freshens your breath.*
- *Improves the quality of your skin.*
- *Aids in weight loss.*
- *Reduces inflammation.*

- *Gives you an energy boost.*
- *Helps your body fight off viral infections—LifeHack[3]*

Sun Tea

Another fun way to add healthy flavor to your drinking water is by making sun tea with it. Sun tea is an old tradition. I can remember my best friend's mother making it on hot summer days back in the seventies. She would use Lipton tea bags back then. But because we're going for healthy hydration here, I recommend using organic caffeine-free tea.

Simply choose a variety of tea that you enjoy, which is also particularly strong in taste, so that you don't have to further flavor it. Personally, I like the mint, ginger, and ginseng teas because their flavors are strong enough to stand alone and they have their own positive health benefits. Attach multiple tea bags (or looseleaf tea in a tea holder) to the top of a glass pitcher filled with pure, clean drinking water. Then set it out in the bright sunlight for an entire day. Let the hot, radiant energy of the sun naturally brew your tea. Serve by pouring it over ice. That's it! That's sun tea!

If you absolutely must add more flavor to your sun tea, then consider adding some lemon juice and/or organic honey, and perhaps even a cinnamon stick or sprig of mint.

---

[3] Krissy Brady, "11 Benefits of Drinking Lemon Water (And How to Drink It for Health)," LifeHack, November 17, 2023, https://www.lifehack.org/articles/lifestyle/11-benefits-lemon-water-you-didnt-know-about.html.

Watery Foods

Another great way to get more fluid into your body is by adding water-laden meals, side dishes, snacks, and even smoothies to your daily meal planning. Refreshing bowls of mixed fruits and vegetables (such as a tomato and cucumber salad, or mixed melons or berries) are delicious and natural ways to hydrate. Plus, you get the added benefits of plant nutrients and fiber. You can also choose to add daily servings of watery soups or bisques to your meals. (Try to forgo heavy seasonings that contain high levels of sugar and salt.) You might also want to make smoothies out of your favorite fruits and vegetables by blending them with ice in a plant-based medium like coconut juice.

Fruits and vegetables are inherently high in fluid content. Once consumed, they break down to release their fluids and serve as an additional source of hydration.

The WRENS – Rest

Getting enough good quality rest on a regular basis is crucial to maintaining your body's overall health and wellness.

It is during times of quality rest that your body, mind, and nervous system have a chance to sort through the wear and tear of everyday life and begin the process of healing, rebalancing, and resetting.

On the flip side of that, if you are cutting adequate amounts of rest out of your daily routine, either because you are undervaluing rest, or because you are trying to be more productive in other areas of your life, or perhaps because something else is going on that is inhibiting your ability to rest properly, then you are most certainly compromising your health to some degree. Eventually, the ill effects of that compromise will show up.

Sleep & Relaxation

There are two forms of rest that your body requires in order to maintain its best overall health. They are: *sleep* and *relaxation.*

Sleep

We all know what sleep is. It's that thing you do when you retire to your bed and allow your everyday life to slip into a kind of stasis. You drift into unconsciousness and eventually into dreamland. Leading up to and during sleep, a hormone called melatonin is released, which signals a host of other sleep-supporting chemical changes in your body. As these changes occur, you find yourself becoming tired and groggy. Eventually, your brain waves alter, and your state of consciousness shifts. That's when you begin releasing tension that has built up in your muscles, nervous system, and brain throughout the day. That's also when your body embarks on a restorative journey as it moves through the various stages of sleep. Eventually, as you continue to sustain sleep, you complete an entire sleep cycle, and then a series of sleep cycles.

When you sleep, sedative-like chemicals are released to tranquilize your voluntary muscle groups so that you remain immobilized during your various stages of sleep. This is especially true in the REM stage, which is the stage of sleep when you do your most active dreaming. Some of these chemical changes limit your ability to sense stimuli in your immediate environment, making it possible for you to move through the stages of sleep without being constantly interrupted and awakened by distractions.

Researchers have observed that almost every living being appears to engage in some form of intermittent sleep-like stasis, and many appear to dream to some extent. Although the science of sleep can still be a bit subjective at times, there seems to be a consensus that most living beings need to engage in some form of a sleep-like state at regular intervals to maintain their healthy physical condition.

In our human bodies, the science of sleep seems fairly clear:

"Sleep plays a critical role in immune function, metabolism, memory, learning, and other vital functions." —Harvard Medical School[4]

"Sleep affects almost every type of tissue and system in the body—from the brain, heart, and lungs to metabolism, immune function, mood, and disease resistance. Research shows that a chronic lack of sleep, or getting poor quality sleep, increases the risk of disorders including high blood pressure, cardiovas-

---

[4] "Why Sleep Matters: Benefits of Sleep," Harvard Medical School: Division of Sleep Medicine, October 1, 2021,
https://sleep.hms.harvard.edu/education-training/public-education/sleep-and-health-education-program/sleep-health-education-41,

[5] "The Benefits of Slumber: Why You Need a Good Night's Sleep," NIH News in Health, April 2013, https://newsinhealth.nih.gov/2013/04/benefits-slumber.

cular disease, diabetes, depression, and obesity."—NIH News in Health[5]

"During sleep, most of the body's systems are in an anabolic state, helping to restore the immune, nervous, skeletal, and muscular systems; these are vital processes that maintain mood, memory, and cognitive function, and play a large role in the function of the endocrine and immune systems." —NIH National Library of Medicine[6]

And there you have it. Virtually every aspect of your physical body is being attended to while you sleep. That means…

The quality of health you are experiencing today has, in many ways, been affected by the quality of sleep you have or have not been getting.

Factors Inhibiting Sleep

Because sleep is so important to your overall health, you would think that falling asleep when your body needs to would come as naturally as breathing. But that's not always the case. There are many factors that can interfere with your body's ability to transition into and sustain quality sleep. In fact, sleep disorders are rather commonplace in today's world.

---

[6] "The role of insufficient sleep and circadian misalignment in obesity," NIH National Library of Medicine, October 24, 2022, https://www.ncbi.nlm.nih.gov/pmc/articles/PMC9590398/.

For one thing, we live in ever complicated and unpredictable times, which generates stress. The cumulative effects of the stress we experience by simply trying to live our lives can wreak havoc on our sleep patterns. Stress leads to anxiety, and anxiety can lead to sleep disorders. Also, traumatic experiences can overstimulate our nervous and endocrine systems, keeping us chronically trapped in a fight-or-flight chemical response, which in turn negatively affects our ability to sleep. Also, environmental factors, which we might not have a lot of control over (such as disruptive noises, light pollution, temperature issues, etc.) can distract us and inhibit our ability to sustain sound, rejuvenating sleep. Illness and pain can inhibit sleep. Additionally, many of the medications intended to treat illness and pain can alter our physical chemistry to the degree that we are unable to fall into or sustain a restful night's sleep.

And, wouldn't you know it, age itself can cause sleep disorders. That's because with age comes diminished hormone activity, and hormones trigger many of the internal chemical changes needed to induce and sustain sleep. It seems a rather cruel twist of fate that just as our aging bodies could use the regenerative attributes of sleep the most, sometimes regenerative sleep can be evasive.

When to Seek Help

If you are experiencing a sleep disorder, then one of the first questions you might want to ask yourself is: *Could there be a medical or psychological condition involved?* If you believe there could be, or if you suspect that a prescribed medication is altering your sleep patterns, then I suggest making an appointment with your most trusted healthcare professional sooner than later. Make sure to choose someone who you can easily communicate with, because it will probably take both of you, working collaboratively, to come up with a solution.

Quality sleep is too important to your overall health and well-being to simply be dismissed.

In addition to seeking help from a trusted professional, there are some life changes you can make right now, on your own, to improve your body's ability to enter into and sustain sleep. Collectively, these changes constitute a sleep routine, which has come to be known as *good sleep hygiene.*

Good Sleep Hygiene

Good sleep hygiene is all about making small but effective life changes that help you get and sustain better quality sleep. The beautiful thing about *good sleep hygiene* is that it really does work by positively affecting the systems in your body that are directly involved with sleep (including your senses, consciousness, subconscious, thought patterns, brain chemistry, nervous system, and endocrine system). *Good sleep hygiene* is something that you can do on your own, without any additional appointments, consultations, approvals, or out-of-pocket expenses to worry about.

According to the CDC (Centers for Disease Control and Prevention), as cited in their article "Tips for Better Sleep," there are some habits you can establish that will improve your body's ability to enter into and sustain sleep:

1. *Be consistent. Go to bed at the same time each night, and get up at the same time each morning, including on the weekends.*

2. *Make sure your bedroom is quiet, dark, relaxing, and at a comfortable temperature.*

217

3. *Remove electronic devices, such as TVs, computers, and smartphones from the bedroom.*

4. *Avoid large meals, caffeine, and alcohol before bedtime.*

5. *Get some exercise. Being physically active during the day can help you fall asleep more easily at night.— Centers for Disease Control and Prevention*[7]

Additional Suggestions

Building on those suggestions, I would like to add a few tips of my own, which I have personally found helpful:

6. *Wear comfortable loose clothing. Don't go to bed wearing anything too tight, irritating, or constricting on your body.*

7. *Keep a to-do list next to your bed. This takes the mental anxiety over what needs to be done out of your brain, and puts it down on paper instead.*

8. *Keep a dream journal. This can make sleeping more of an adventure and less of a task. You might even discover some interesting insights into yourself and your life as a result.*

---

[7] "Tips for Better Sleep," Centers for Disease Control and Prevention, September 13, 2022,
https://www.cdc.gov/sleep/about_sleep/sleep_hygiene.html.

9. *Consider meditation. Meditation is a practice by which you intentionally relax your body and mind in order to transition into another state of consciousness. Some studies have found that this practice creates a kind of dexterity for being able to transition into sleep as well.*

Relaxation

Relaxation is another form of rest that both your body and mind require. While sleep is a passive experience that involves a respite from your everyday task-driven life and a surrender of consciousness, relaxation (as I am referring to it here) is a horse of a different color. Relaxation still involves a respite from your everyday task-driven life, but it's a respite you can engage in while remaining alert.

Relaxation, like sleep, is a respite from your everyday task-driven life that allows your body and mind to release stored-up tension. Relaxation, however, doesn't require your body's complete immobilization and surrender of consciousness. Relaxation is a consciously present experience that can, in fact, be quite active.

Relaxation is a form of self-care that can be achieved through calming activities (such as birdwatching, enjoying a beverage, working on a puzzle, listening to music, etc.), or through more vigorous activities (such as hiking, swimming, running, exercising, etc.). However you choose to relax, what makes it a truly relaxing experience for you is that you enjoy doing it, and that it ultimately releases tension from your body and mind.

"As important as it is to have a plan for doing work, it is perhaps more important to plan for rest, relaxation, self-care, and sleep." —Akiroq Brost

Sleep and relaxation are two sides of the same coin. Both are important for your overall good health and sense of well-being; both help to regulate your mood, metabolism, heart rate, etc.; and both improve your brain's health and relieve stress. Therefore, a healthy blend of both sleep and relaxing activities should be a part of your holistic health plan.

The WRENS – Exercise

The First Law of Motion states that…

"Every object will remain at rest or in uniform motion in a straight line, unless compelled to change its state by the action of an external force."—Sir Isaac Newton

A more commonly used sentiment, based on this same law, goes something like this:

"A body in motion stays in motion, whereas a body at rest stays at rest."

Animation vs. Inertia

Self-animation (or movement) is one of the components that define life. When a living being demonstrates a lack of movement, in a best-case scenario, it can be assumed that it is resting, which is necessary for maintaining its health and well-being. But a reduction in animation outside of adequate rest and recovery can be a predictor of physical decline. If a living being lingers too long in a state of sluggishness, it can, over time, enter a state of inertia, in which case its vital life force is paused and could be poised for decline. Once a living being's life force declines to the point where it's depleted, it will die, and it will be inanimate.

Assuming that the Law of Attraction and Sir Issac Newton's First Law of Movement are both valid, then it stands to reason that by choosing to act on your own personal inertia by engaging in some form of intentional increased movement, you may be able to reverse your inertia and begin increasing your available life force again.

If your body has had its adequate measure of rest for healing and rejuvenation purposes, then it must balance that out with renewed animation to remain healthy and engaged in life.

Exercise is a chosen form of animation. It can be that interrupting force Newton was referring to.

If you think of time as a currency that buys you more opportunities to experience life, then you can think of exercise as a currency that buys you more time.

Body, Mind & Spirit

I use the phrase *"body, mind, and spirit"* a lot in this book, but more so in this chapter because, as far as health is concerned, one so obviously influences the others.

Each area of your life—body, mind, and spirit—supports and enhances the others. If any one of these areas is compromised, your overall health suffers.

Let's delve further into these three areas, and more specifically, how exercising each of them can help improve your overall health.

Exercising the Body

You exercise your body by moving your body.

Physical exercise is, without a doubt, a cornerstone in the foundation of good health. Besides keeping the body fit today, it helps you navigate the aging process with more energy, functionality, and grace.

"Exercise boosts energy. Regular physical activity can improve your muscle strength and boost your endurance. Exercise sends oxygen and nutrients to your tissues and helps your cardiovascular system work more efficiently. And when your heart and lung health improve, you have more energy to tackle daily chores." —Mayo Clinic [8]

The Three S's

There are basically three categories of exercise that help you maintain your body in good working condition. I like to refer to them as the *three S's*. They are exercises for *suppleness, strength*, and *stamina*.

Suppleness

Exercises for physical suppleness include gentle, fluid motions that encourage your body to maintain its flexibility and preserve its range of motion.

---

[8] "Exercise: 7 benefits of regular physical activity," Mayo Clinic, https://www.mayoclinic.org/healthy-lifestyle/fitness/in-depth/exercise/art-20048389.

If you allow your body to become too lax from lack of use, then when you do push yourself to do something more physical, you could experience resistance and pain. Pushing through physical resistance and pain can cause your cortisol levels to spike and your blood pressure to rise. It can even result in physical injury. Therefore, it's important to engage in strategic exercises that help your body maintain its suppleness as much as possible, for as long as you can, so that you don't lose the ability to do so prematurely.

Exercises for Suppleness

Gentle Yoga – Gentle yoga is yoga that is low in intensity. The poses you want to focus on are specifically designed to promote suppleness in the body. They include slow, easy bends, stretches, and twists.

Walking – Walking regularly helps your body to manage its balance and gait. It gently forces more blood flow into the *stuck* areas of your body, while moving and strengthening the muscles, tendons, and ligaments that support your bones and joints. All of this benefits the general health of your body and helps it to maintain its overall suppleness.

Dancing – Dancing is a blend of both fitness and fun! Dancing has also been proven to improve the body's gait and balance, which leads to more suppleness in movement in general. Dancing stimulates your entire body. It increases your oxygen intake and raises your heart rate. Dancing also triggers the release of serotonin and endorphins, which are good for your body and brain.

"Dance also has physical and cognitive benefits that may exceed those of other forms of exercise." —*Harvard Health Publishing*[9]

Strength

Exercising for strength involves pushing and/or pulling your body against some form of resistance. You need physical strength to maintain your body's mobility and functionality throughout your life.

I'm not talking about bulking up or acquiring that perfect beach body (unless that's what you want to do!), but it is important to maintain as much strength in your legs, arms, back, and neck as you can, so that these things don't grow too weak and start to falter over time.

Exercises for Strength

Beginner, Intermediate, or Advanced Yoga – The beautiful thing about yoga is that it can be tailored to any skill level; you don't need special equipment or tools to do it; it can be done just about anywhere, anytime; and you can choose poses designed for a specific result, which in this case would be strength.

---

[9] "Let's dance! Rhythmic motion can improve your health," Harvard Health Publishing, April 21, 2016, https://www.health.harvard.edu/blog/lets-dance-rhythmic-motion-can-improve-your-health-201604219468.

Resistance Training – Resistance training is another way to strengthen your muscles by requiring them to push and/or pull against weight and/or gravity. This type of exercise could include doing things like sit-ups, push-ups, squats, presses, and lunges. It can also include the use of tools, such as dumbbells, kettlebells, resistance bands, and exercise equipment.

Walking – Walking works to increase strength because it raises your body's oxygen levels and increases blood flow to many of the muscle groups you use in everyday life, including those that support your feet, ankles, knees, hips, and back.

Stamina

Exercising for stamina involves moving your body over a set period of time, then extending that movement and/or time frame beyond your comfort level. This helps to increase your endurance level and maintain your available energy needed for doing everyday things with more ease.

Over time, your body incrementally loses its stamina, and you start requiring more rest and recovery time after physical exertion. This means that aging requires a somewhat delicate balance between resting and movement. On the one hand, you need to honor your physical reality and give your body the adequate rest and recovery time it needs to maintain its good health. On the other hand, you need to resist the urge to stay too lethargic for too long. Failure to rest can lead to physical and mental burnout, stress, and even injury, whereas resting too much can lead to a sedimentary lifestyle, which predictably leads to physical decline and the loss of stamina.

Becoming overly inert can lead to a lack of stamina and difficulty doing everyday things.

The good news is: maintaining your body's stamina isn't so hard to do. It basically boils down to remaining active.

<u>*Exercises for Stamina*</u>

High-Intensity Yoga – As mentioned earlier, there are different forms of yoga. Yoga can be done gently or vigorously. If you want to use yoga to increase stamina, then you'll want to do longer, more vigorous workouts, and you'll want to choose workouts and time frames that push you beyond your comfort level. Over time, this should work to increase your body's endurance level.

Doing Things the Hard Way – This is one of the simplest things you can do to increase your body's overall stamina. You don't need any special equipment or skillset to do it. You just need to choose to do some things the hard way, versus always opting for ease. When it comes to activities like visiting a friend who lives a couple blocks away, or getting to the upper level in a building, or parking at the store, don't always choose the easy way. If you can, walk the couple of blocks, climb the stairs, and park further away from the store's entrance. By forcing your body to take these extra steps, and by refusing to always make things easy on yourself, you can increase your overall physical stamina and have more energy available to you for doing everyday tasks.

High-Intensity Activities – By engaging in activities like running, jogging, swimming, hiking, biking, or sports, you will regularly increase your body's heart rate and blood flow, and subsequently your overall health and stamina.

Plus, these activities are stimulating and, as such, they prompt your body to produce endorphins. Endorphins offer a whole other set of health benefits, such as enhancing your sense of pleasure, staving off depression, reducing stress and pain, and helping to balance your brain's chemistry.

Walking – Walking is simply good for your health in general. It utilizes almost all your muscle groups, increases blood flow and heart rate, and promotes a greater sense of balance. That said, when you increase the intensity of your walks by walking briskly and/or for an extended period of time, you are also helping to increase your body's overall stamina.

Massage

Although technically not an exercise, massage is something you can do in conjunction with exercise to enhance the results.

Our bodies are designed to be stimulated by touch. Massage is a form of healing touch that benefits the entire body.

Massage enhances the benefits of physical exercise by gently stimulating the nerve receptors that respond to touch, and by increasing blood flow. It can also help move lymphatic fluid. Getting a good, deep massage (now and again) can release tension and stress being held in your body. It can also help to release tight and knotted muscles and tendons, which can, over time, lead to stiffness, pain, incorrect muscle memory, skeletal displacement, and even poor posture.

"Massage therapy is safe and effective for people of all ages. It's not only a feel-good way to indulge or pamper yourself. It's a powerful tool to help you take charge of your health

and well-being, whether you have a specific health condition or are looking for a stress reliever." —Mayo Clinic Health System [10]

You can go to a professional masseuse for your muscle massage, or you can try self-massaging your muscles in the privacy of your home by using tools designed for this purpose.

There are three massage tools, which I have personally used, and can attest to that they work (although results may vary depending on your specific conditions). They are the:

- Handheld electric deep tissue massager
- Muscle massage ball
- Muscle massage roller with tread

When using either a muscle massage ball or roller with tread (my personal favorite), simply lie on the floor with the device under the muscles you're targeting, then gently push and roll your body over the device. As you get more comfortable doing this, you can push the targeted areas harder against the device. This will start to give you a deeper tissue massage. Over time, this technique can help to loosen up some of those tight, knotted muscles, giving you more flexibility and restoring blood flow to those areas.

"Massage with a roller device reduces muscle soreness and is accompanied by a higher PPT (Package Power in

---

[10] Ivy Conrad, "Benefits of massage therapy," Mayo Clinic Health System, March 22, 2022, https://www.mayoclinichealthsystem.org/hometown-health/speaking-of-health/benefits-of-massage-therapy.

Watts) of the affected muscle." —*NIH National Library of Medicine*[11]

Keeping It Simple

Exercising the body doesn't have to be overly complicated. I recommend having a baseline routine that's easy to incorporate into your daily routine, then adding to it as you are able.

Personally, I've put together an eleven-minute yoga routine, which I knock out in the mornings after my coffee and before getting dressed for the day. Then I take a walk after dinner. That's it. That's my baseline. I may do additional things above and beyond that, or I may not. The point is: my baseline is simple enough to maintain, and it's helping me to stay in better health.

"Simplicity is the key to brilliance." —*Bruce Lee*

Exercising the Mind

You exercise your mind by challenging and stimulating your brain.

There's no doubt about it, in order to stay fit as the years tick by, your body needs to stay engaged in life. The same holds true for your brain. One of the worst things you can do

---

[11] "Specific and cross over effects of massage for muscle soreness, trial," NIH National Library of Medicine, February 2014, https://pubmed.ncbi.nlm.nih.gov/24567859/.

for your brain's health is to allow it to grow too lax or lazy over time. There are many factors that contribute to a mental decline as we age, and a tendency towards lazy thinking is surely one of them. It's also one that can be addressed.

"A lazy brain is a shrinking brain. Those who don't engage in complex mental activity over their lifetime have twice the shrinkage in a key part of the brain in old age. "—UNSW Sydney [12]

Complex mental activity is activity that challenges and stimulates your brain. It's activity that requires you to go above and beyond the urge to simply get by on what you already know, while shirking opportunities to learn new things and expand your mind.

As comfortable as familiarity is, it can be harmful for your mental health if it limits your potential for mental growth, stimulation, and expansion.

Just as there are activities that you can engage in to exercise your body, there are ways to exercise your brain as well.

Exercises for the Brain

Staying Engaged – Whether it's working, volunteering, visiting, creating, exploring, etc., you should try to stay engaged in this world. When you are engaged in life, both your body and brain are stimulated in a million different

---

[12] "A lazy brain is a shrinking brain," UNSW Sydney, July 22, 2008, https://newsroom.unsw.edu.au/news/health/lazy-brain-shrinking-brain.

ways. Serotonin, endorphins, and dopamine are released, which help to balance your brain's chemistry as well as lift your mood.

Reading – Besides entertaining you, reading stimulates your imagination, enhances your visualization skills, and improves your focus and your brain's connectivity. It's also known to reduce stress, and is being studied for its role in reducing the odds of developing Alzheimer's.

Learning – Learning new things should be a lifelong endeavor. Go back to school. Take a class at the local college. Take an online master class. Read something educational. There are so many fascinating subjects out there to explore. Pick one and start learning more about it. Learning disciplines your brain. It forces it to focus and build neuropathways as it takes in and assimilates new information and understanding.

Starting Something New – Maybe it's a new creative project, or moving to a new location, or getting a new job. However you decide to do it, starting something new introduces fresh, vibrant energy into your world and forces your brain to figure new stuff out. New experiences challenge and stimulate your brain in ways that living day after day, year after year, or even decade after decade in redundancy won't.

Doing Mental Exercises – Card games, word games, puzzles… These things challenge the brain to look for patterns and solutions, and to strategize.

Walking – As mentioned earlier, walking is simply good for your health in general. Your brain's health is no exception. Walking is a movement that both stimulates and relaxes your brain. Walking requires balance and coordination, which are managed in the cerebellum, a part of your brain that also plays an important role in cognitive function, language, and memory. You raise your heart rate when you walk, which increases blood flow and oxygen to your brain. Your senses are activated when you walk. Sights, smells, and physical sensations become data from the outside world that your brain takes in and works to makes sense of. Walking triggers your instincts and heightens your awareness in a way that sitting comfortably in familiar spaces will not.

Sunrises

"Brave Helios, wake up your steeds.
Bring the warmth the countryside needs."
—The Moody Blues, "The Day Begins"

The countryside isn't the only thing that needs the warm, life-affirming light of the sun. Our brains need it as well.

We are living, organic beings on a living, organic planet. As such, our bodies require the elements of this Earth to remain balanced and healthy. These elements include the Earth's air, water, sun, soil, plants, and animals, as well as her seasons and cycles. Yet because of the way we've structured our societies, and the advances we've made in technology (which include the creation of artificial environments), many of us have fallen out of rhythm with the natural cycles of this planet and, in particular, with the natural cycle of light to darkness.

The timing and ratio of light to darkness you experience during a twenty-four-hour period is known as your circadian rhythm. When your circadian rhythm varies too much from what your brain was designed to function by, it can negatively affect your mental health.

A beautiful way to reharmonize your brain's circadian rhythm with its natural environment is to watch sunrises. (IMPORTANT NOTE: You can look towards, but never directly at the sun. Looking directly at the sun will cause serious damage to your eyes.) When you watch the sunrise, your brain is flooded with healthy chemicals triggered by the growing light. That said, if you're like me, and are rarely up to see sunrises (I write well into the night and often miss sunrises), then when you do wake up, you can still go outside, look up at the sky, and with your hand covering the directness of the sun, gaze at the blue sky to the side of the sun. Try holding your gaze on the sky for about one minute.

The first time I tried this as a conscious exercise, one of my investments was tanking. I was profoundly worried about it at the time. However, after a few seconds of gazing indirectly at the morning sunlight, something in me shifted. I found myself becoming more optimistic about my day ahead. My financial stressor was still in place, but I was more confident that I could handle it. That's a pretty powerful shift as far as I'm concerned, and I believe it was due to the chemical changes in my brain activated by the natural light.

Watching sunrises, when done safely, is good medicine for your brain. It helps to reset your circadian rhythm, which in turn should help you sleep better, especially when you follow the *good sleep hygiene* habits outlined earlier in this chapter.

"Viewing sunlight in the morning causes ~50 percent increase in circulating cortisol, epinephrine, and dopamine.

233

These leverage healthy increases in energy, immune system function and mood." —*Andrew D. Huberman, X* [13]

Your Brain & Your Personal Autonomy

If you want to remain standing in your personal power and autonomy as you move through time, then I recommend looking after your brain's health, just as you would any other aspect of your physical health. Some things may be beyond your personal ability to control when it comes to health matters, but other things you can control, at least to a degree. It's important to do what you can today to keep your brain healthy, active, and engaged, thereby increasing the odds that you will remain autonomous in your own life for years to come.

You can lose physical function and still work around that to some degree with tools and various compensation techniques. But a mental decline will eventually rob you of your independence.

Look, you are *starting over* again in life and, as such, you have an opportunity to try new things and have some exciting new experiences! Don't miss out on those experiences because it became too easy to rest in mental apathy and thereby develop a lazy mind. Of course, you will need to rest your mind from time to time so that your brain can recover from stress and reestablish its chemical equilibrium and overall good health.

---

[13] Andrew D. Huberman, X, August 3, 2022,
https://twitter.com/hubermanlab/status/1554854275225776128?lang=en.

But you don't want to linger too long in a state of mental apathy. Your brain will suffer if you do. As you are able, seek out ways to keep your brain stimulated and your mind sharp. That way, you can go into your next chapter in life as fully empowered and engaged as possible.

Exercising the Spirit

You exercise your spirit through your connections.

Spirit, as I'm referring to it here, is the part of you that exists beyond the physical. It's the energy, essence, consciousness, and individuality you came into this world with, and it's the energy, essence, consciousness, and individuality you will leave with. Your spirit is your truth. It's your authentic self. It can be influenced and shaped by your life experiences, but it remains individually you before, during, and after your time here in the physical world.

> *"We are not human beings having a spiritual experience. We are spiritual beings having a human experience."*
> —Pierre Teilhard de Chardin

Your spirit is your life spark, your ongoing consciousness, and the essence of who you are.

As you move forward on your journey, your spirit will have needs just as your body and mind do. Your spirit can remain vibrant, strong, and healthy throughout your life, or it can grow dim, weak, and repressed. Knowing this, what can you do to ensure the former? What can you do to keep your spirit vibrant, strong, and healthy? Well, your spirit is strengthened by your connections, and, in particular, by your connection with *love, joy, truth, purpose, nature,* and *your higher power.*

If you can maintain your connection with love, joy, truth, purpose, nature, and your higher power, then, whatever else you may or may not accomplish in this lifetime, all will be well at your core spiritual self.

Let's take a deeper look into your spiritual needs by looking at some of the ways you can exercise (or engage) them.

Exercises for the Spirit

Connecting with Love – Your heart must remain open for your spirit to thrive. Make an effort to love, honor, and cherish others, so that your love can continue to exercise and enhance your spirit. Love is about loving. Although desirable, love doesn't have to be reciprocated to enhance your spirit. When in the throes of heartbreak or unrequited love, try to remember that everything in this physical world is temporary, and that includes the physical presence of those you love. Your heart really can endure the pain of loss because you came into this world to love, and loving often comes hand in hand with loss. But if you can retain a true and loving heart, even when it hurts like the dickens to do so, then you can retain your true and loving and, therefore, healthy spirit.

Connecting with Joy – In a material world, we often struggle with the survival process. Threats to our well-being seem to lurk around every corner, making it easy to slip out of joy and into fight-or-flight mode instead. That said, taking time to still experience joy, even in the worst of times, needs to remain a spiritual priority. Joy exercises and fortifies your spirit, even on the bleakest of days. So, whatever else you're going through at the time, remember to appreciate that sunset. Enjoy your favorite meal. Spend a special moment with someone you love and enjoy

236

spending time with. Joyful experiences feed your soul and exercise your spirit. Joyful experiences are often described as *lifting your spirit* for a reason.

Connecting with Truth – Sometimes we dodge the truth because we believe a falsity will serve us better. But the truth is, your truth is always good enough. That's worth repeating!

Your truth is always good enough!

Your spiritual self is not a false self. It's who you intrinsically are. Therefore, by committing to always speak and live by your truth, even when it's sometimes painful to do so, even when there are consequences involved, you validate your true self. Speaking your truth means being honest and forthright in your communications. It also means living, working, and planning your future authentically, in ways that resonate with your spirit. Your commitment to truth will exercise your spirit and strengthen its constitution.

Connecting with Purpose – Whether it's serving your family or your community; or whether it's employing a talent or expressing your authentic self; or whether you're advancing a cause or simply committed to being a positive role model in some way; when you identify a greater purpose to your life (something greater than just fulfilling your own needs), your spirit is exercised and doing what it came into this world to do. Having a sense of purpose greatly enhances the health and wellness of your spirit.

Connecting with Nature – Nature, when left alone, unfolds in perfect order. Its energies are perfectly aligned and exist purely as they were designed to. *Like attracts* *like*. So, in that sense, by finding ways to connect with the natural world, you can begin to align your own energy into a more perfect and pure order as well. Nature helps to balance and restore your spiritual energy.

Connecting with Your Higher Power – Whether it's God or the Universe; or whether you believe in a higher power in the context of a religion or something less defined; or even if you simply believe in the wisdom of your higher self; by acknowledging something greater than yourself and connecting with that source, your spirit regains its sense of peace. It remembers what it has always known: that there is a perfect order to your life.

The Old Cowboy

Just this past week, as I was walking in the mountains, I happened upon an elderly gentleman walking on the trail towards me. As we approached each other, he stepped aside and leaned against his walking stick. He said, "You'll have to excuse me, I'm a little tired."

I responded by saying, "That's okay, we all get a little tired at times. At least you're out here enjoying nature." That's when we chitchatted a bit, and he opened up and told me this story:

He said that he had been a cowboy by trade, and that he had often driven cattle through these very mountains. He said that he missed the mountains and wanted to experience them once again. He told me that he was a Jehovah's Witness and, as such, he had been taught to appreciate nature. He quoted this Bible verse:

"I will lift up my eyes unto the hills

He then went on to tell me an even more personal story:

He said his wife had recently died of ovarian cancer, and that he missed her terribly and had some regrets about the way he treated her over the years. He told me they were married at a time when women were taught to defer their needs to their husband's, and, regretfully, he took advantage of that. He confessed to brushing many of her needs and desires aside as unimportant. When she was still alive, she wanted a palomino horse. She wanted to go riding with him in the mountains. But that never happened because he never got around to getting her the horse. He told me that during his walk, he had asked God for another chance with his wife. He asked for another opportunity to ride with her in the mountains and show her just how beautiful they really were.

I responded to him by saying something like, "I'm certain you'll get to see her again."

And he replied, "You don't understand. I want another chance with her here, in this place. I want to give her the horse and take her into these very mountains. I want her to feel this wind, and hear these birds, and breathe this air."

I didn't know what to say at that point. I didn't know how to comfort him. With a tear in his eye, he told me he needed to go and let me get on with my walk, before I ran out of light. I wished him a good evening, and we went our separate ways.

It was certainly serendipitous that I ran into this gentleman when I did because I was writing this chapter at the time. The cowboy in the story above seems to have been connected with his spiritual need for joy, purpose, and nature when he was out on the land doing his thing. By his own account, he was connected with his higher power, his Jehovah. But for whatever reason, he had remained largely disconnected from his truth and his love when it came to his wife. Because of this, his spirit was experiencing regret in his final days. I can only hope that when truth and love finally resurfaced in him, as painful as it may have been at the time, they completed his spiritual needs and restored him to whole again.

It's been my observation that...

End-of-life regrets rarely result from one's connection with love, joy, purpose, truth, nature, and a higher power, but rather a disconnection from any one of these things.

The WRENS – Nutrition

"You are what you eat." We've all heard this little snippet of wisdom. But those five little words pack a wallop of truth.

Your body attempts to break down everything you ingest, and then utilizes it for energy, growth, function, and cellular turnover. If you fail to give your body the proper nutrition it needs to do these things, then, sooner or later, your health will be compromised. Count on it!

Something my grandmother used to say when she was trying to get me to eat better was "The soup is only as good or bad as the ingredients you put in it." Metaphorically speaking, she was trying to say that I was the soup, and the foods I ate were the ingredients. It was her rather simplified way of trying to get a child to understand the concept of good nutrition. It worked! To this day, I catch myself thinking about that phrase whenever

I'm picking out groceries, ordering out, or putting together a meal. I may not always adhere to it, but I think about it!

Clean Eating

Something you can do to help ensure that your body gets better nutrition is *clean eating*. Clean eating is basically committing to foods, beverages, spices, and seasonings that are whole and unprocessed, or are a combination of whole and unprocessed foods. This means no chemical preservatives, artificial flavoring (including flavor enhancers), or artificial coloring.

Think of it this way:

When picking out your food, if you could potentially grow, harvest, gather, hunt, or farm it as it is, then it is probably an acceptable item for clean eating.

Clean eating doesn't mean compromising on flavor. For one thing, there are plenty of sauces and spice combinations available today at your local grocery store that are comprised of whole ingredients with no additives, flavor enhancers, or preservatives. If you're not doing so already, I recommend getting into the habit of reading the ingredients in your food sources so that you can identify the cleanest brands and then stick with them. I also recommend learning how to put together meals using whole ingredients.

Learning to cook clean may be challenging at first, but it is also incredibly rewarding! Once you get the hang of it, you'll be proud of your newfound culinary skills and your meals will be delicious and nutritious!

Personally Speaking

Over the years, I've been diagnosed with several chronic health conditions, including lupus and thyroid disease. Each condition, when it's flaring up, tends to trigger another, causing a rather complex domino effect of health issues, which are often difficult to untangle, diagnose, treat, and recover from. I've learned the hard way that adhering to a poor diet will absolutely trigger a chain reaction of ill health in my body. This has made me a big fan of clean eating. I can eat a sugary dessert or a heavily processed meal once in a while and still be okay. But too many consecutive days of sloppy eating will predictably lead to me not feeling well. And, if I slip into a lupus flare-up, due in part to poor eating habits, then it can take me up to six months to pull out of it again. That's how sensitive I am now to what I put in my body.

I might be more sensitive than the average person (consider me a canary in the coal mine as far as food sensitivity goes), but on some level, your body is responding to your diet as well. Over time, the harm caused by poor nutritional sources will show up, whether you're immediately sensitive to it or not.

Your body breaks down all edible food for immediate energy and available nutrients. In that sense, all edible food can seem satisfying in the moment. But in the long term, your ongoing diet will act as either poison or medicine for your overall health.

Gardening

Consider growing your own herb and spice garden, and a vegetable garden as well (if you can manage it). If you live in a condo or apartment, then consider a container garden on your balcony, or a grow station inside your home. (Indoor grow stations are becoming increasingly popular, and they can be easily found online.) You don't need a lot of space to have a little something fresh to add to your meals. Preparing your meals with freshly grown herbs, spices, and vegetables adds amazing flavor that nothing bought at the grocery store can compare to.

When you eat something fresh from the land, you get the full measure of flavors, nutrients, and even medicinal properties that come from consuming freshly harvested clean food.

Gardening can be immensely rewarding once you get into it. Working with living plants focuses your attention and grounds your energy. It's incredibly rewarding to plant, tend, and observe your garden growing and turning into food!

Going Organic

You might also want to consider going organic, especially with your fruits and vegetables, to reduce your exposure to pesticides. If that's not an option (I know organic can be expensive and the options limited), then consider soaking your fruits and vegetables once you get them home to loosen up any chemical applications, then rinse them thoroughly and dry before storing. This may or may not remove everything toxic, but at least it will reduce some of your exposure to pesticides.

Variety

Another thing you can do to help ensure that your body is getting the nutrients it needs is to include a variety of foods in your daily meal planning.

According to the USDA, there are five food groups that we should be pulling from daily to help ensure adequate nutrition. The information below is taken from their website:

1. *Fruits: Includes fruit, one hundred percent fruit juice (preferably with no sugar added, if you're eating clean), berries, melons*

2. *Vegetables: Includes green and dark green vegetables, red, yellow, and orange vegetables, starchy vegetables, beans, peas, and lentils*

3. *Grains: Includes whole grains and refined grains (you'll want to limit refined grains if you're eating clean)*

4. *Protein: Includes meats, poultry, beans, peas, and lentils, nuts, seeds, soy-based foods, seafood, eggs*

5. *Dairy: Includes milks, non-dairy calcium alternatives (like coconut, soy, and almond milks), yogurt, cheese—U. S. Department of Agriculture[14]*

MyPlate.Gov

At www.myplate.gov, there's an overview of each of the food groups. This site also gives advice on how to substitute certain foods if you're following a specialty diet (such as paleo, vegetarian, gluten-free, keto, etc.) to help ensure that you are still getting the variety of nutrients your body requires.

---

[14] Sarah Chang and Kristin Koegel, "Back to Basics: All About MyPlate Food Groups," U.S. Department of Agriculture, September 26, 2017, https://www.usda.gov/media/blog/2017/09/26/back-basics-all-about-myplate-food-groups.

Eating the Rainbow

Eating the rainbow is another way to help ensure that your body is getting the variety of nutrients it requires.

"Eating the rainbow" refers to adding a variety of colors, aromas, and flavors to your meals.

Not only do colorful meals provide an attractive culinary presentation (ta-da!), but a variety of colors can indicate a variety of nutritional attributes as well. Natural food sources contain something called phytochemicals. Different phytochemicals result in foods having different colors to them, as well as different nutritional benefits.

According to an article published by the Mayo Clinic, eating a variety of foods with different phytochemicals in them can help you achieve:

- *Improved vision*
- *Degreased inflammation*
- *Reduced risk of chronic diseases, including cancer, heart disease, and diabetes*
- *A strengthened immune system—Mayo Clinic*[15]

I suggest to anyone interested in having a variety of nutrients in their meals, that they Google and print one of the many *"Eating the Rainbow"* charts out there and post it in their

---

[15] Joel Streed, "Eat the rainbow for good health," Mayo Clinic, July 21, 2022, https://newsnetwork.mayoclinic.org/discussion/eat-the-rainbow-for-good-health/.

kitchen. These charts will vary a bit (depending on their source), but they will all offer a basic outline of the nutritional properties found in different food colors, based on their phytochemicals.

Below, I've done a brief breakdown of the different food colors, along with a generalization of their nutritional offerings (although there is so much more than what I'm listing here):

Nutritional Benefits Based on Phytochemicals

- *Red = benefits to heart and blood*
- *Orange and yellow = benefits to eyes, skin, and recovery*
- *Green = benefits to bones and immune system*
- *Blue and purple = benefits to brain*
- *Brown and white = benefits to energy and strength*

Say a Little Prayer

You're probably aware of the practice of saying grace before meals. Saying grace is typically a religious practice that thanks God for the food about to be received. But you don't have to subscribe to a particular religion, or even be religious at all, to have and express gratitude for your meals. I recommend pausing before each meal to give thanks for that meal, because gratitude is a superpower that shifts and improves energy, including the energy your body uses to consume and digest your meals.

I'm also going to suggest that you try adding another dimension to your expression of gratitude by including some *intention*. Besides nourishment, you can ask God (or the Universe, or your body, or even the food itself) to apply some of the food's nutritional offerings towards a specific task, such as healing or strengthening. When you add intention to your meals, you begin to eat more consciously. This changes your relationship with food. Eating is no longer just about satiating hunger or desire; it becomes an opportunity to set a better intention for your health.

Think of it this way:

Giving thanks for your food puts you in a state of gratitude, and gratitude is a superpower; it has the power to shift energy for the better. Intention is a superpower as well; it has the power to direct energy.

Everything is energy. Your food is energy. Your body is energy. Your higher power is energy. Your digestion and distribution of nutrients is an energetic process. Your intention is energy. Your words have the same energetic frequency as your intention. It's the energy that gets through. It's the energy that's understood by all things.

"Everything is energy and that's all there is to it. Match the frequency of the reality you want, and you cannot help but get that reality. It can be no other way. This is not philosophy. This is physics."—Albert Einstein

It's Not Just About Food

What you consume and assimilate isn't just about food. You have an energic body as well. Your energy can be either nourished or malnourished. It can be healthy or toxic.

What you do... what you say... what you listen to... what and whom you surround yourself with... these things are absorbed into your energy field and affect you.

Like attracts like is the basis for the Law of Attraction. This law works on an energetic level. If your environment (which is always affecting your personal energy to some degree) doesn't match the frequency of what you're trying to attract in your life (and this includes the state of your health), then you're going to have to make some changes or give up on your aspirations. *"This is not philosophy. This is physics."*

The WRENS – Support

Getting adequate measures of water, rest, exercise, and nutrition to improve and maintain your overall health is something that's always within your power to do. But sometimes, these things aren't enough. Sometimes, other forces show up in your life that negatively impact your health, and it becomes beyond your ability to deal with them on your own.

No one is immortal. Regardless of how well you try to take care of yourself, you are still susceptible to developing health issues that are beyond your personal ability to manage. That's when you need to look outside of yourself for additional support.

Nutritional Supplements

There's a common belief that if you just get the right nutrition from your diet, you will never need to take any kind of supplement. I don't believe that's realistic in today's world. For one thing, we live longer. As our bodies age, various health issues arise that can at least be partially corrected through dietary supplementation. In addition, our modern food supply is lacking the full nutritional value that it once held. There are also substances in our food and environment today that cause inflammation and block cell receptors, reducing our ability to absorb certain nutrients at a cellular level. Health conditions, as well as the medications issued to treat them, can sometimes inhibit the body's ability to utilize the nutrition it is receiving, as well as how efficiently the body can produce certain substances needed to self-regulate and regenerate itself. In all these instances, certain over-the-counter supplements may be helpful.

Down the Rabbit Hole

When my health fell apart a few years ago, I was sent down a rabbit hole of lab work, imaging, and referrals. As clinically evident conditions began to come to light, some of my physicians suggested over-the-counter supplements in addition to whatever other treatment plans they were recommending. Apparently, autoimmune disorders, as well as thyroid disorders (and really, anything negatively affecting the endocrine system), often go hand in hand with certain nutritional deficiencies and electrolyte imbalances. My body wasn't just suffering from the ill effects of the health disorders, but also from the deficiencies that came with them. Once the appropriate supplements were coupled with my other treatment plans, my quality of life improved exponentially.

So, how do you navigate the thousands upon thousands of supplements out there, as well as all the hype and unrealistic expectations that come with them? It's going to be somewhat of a journey to figure out, that's for sure. If you are seeking to add over-the-counter supplements to your healthcare regimen, then be prepared to do some experimentation. That said, you can start your journey off on the right foot by inviting your most trusted healthcare professional along with you, at least in the beginning. A healthcare professional can help you discover where you are clinically deficient, and that's a good place to start when navigating the vast universe of supplements.

Tips for Exploring Over-the-Counter Supplements

Below, I've listed some tips you might want to consider when beginning to explore the benefits of over-the-counter supplements:

1. **Request Lab Work** – Consider making an appointment with a healthcare professional to request that nutritional lab work be ordered. You'll want to ask that person to check for deficiencies in vitamins, nutrients, and micronutrients, as well as hormonal imbalances. Based on those results, your healthcare professional can recommend any appropriate supplements that they think will help correct your deficiencies. (You will probably, at some point, want to go above and beyond this step when adding supplements to your healthcare regimen. But this is a good first step.)

2. **Request a Nutritionist** – You may want to ask your healthcare professional for a referral to a nutritionist. If you have any preexisting condition on record at all, then that condition can be used to justify the referral. Having your lab work in hand when you go to a nutritionist will greatly aid that person in putting together a nutritional plan for you, along with any over-the-counter supplementation that they deem helpful.

3. **Consider Functional Medicine** – Functional medicine is a specialized field of medicine that takes a more holistic approach to healthcare. These practitioners have the same medical training that all medical doctors do (in fact, many of them also serve as general practitioners), but they are additionally trained to look at the body as a whole. They

are often more open to alternative forms of healing, and they can be well-versed in over-the-counter supplements.

4. **Do Your Own Research** – There is so much information and research out there, one healthcare professional can't possibly be up to date on all of it. So, read up on your health conditions and look for the recommended supplements that might help treat them. Just be sure to run those recommendations by your most trusted healthcare professional first. Even if they can't necessarily condone a treatment outside of their scope of expertise, they can at least cross-reference your supplements with your current conditions and medications, so that you can begin to experiment with them safely.

What's Up, Doc?

Another type of support you will need to turn to from time to time, regardless of how well you take care of yourself, is professional medical support.

Sometimes, you just need to go see your doctor.

Challenges within the Healthcare System

If you're an old-timer like me, then you might remember the days when your doctors were trusted friends, confidants, and collaborators. They most likely lived in the same community you lived in, they dined at the same restaurants, and they sent their kids to the same schools. You probably looked up to your doctors and trusted their recommendations unquestioningly, because you knew that their number-one objective was to get you feeling better and functioning again. You had confidence in your doctors. There was a sacred relationship of trust between you and your doctors.

Unfortunately, for the most part, those days are gone. Over the past twenty years or so, the healthcare environment has undergone massive changes, and not all of them for the better. For all the scientific advancements made in the understanding and treatment of health issues, I'm going to guess there are now just as many roadblocks to actually getting that understanding and care. In fact, today, I believe there are more challenges than ever to simply receiving an accurate diagnosis and treatment.

So, what has happened in our modern-day healthcare system that can potentially prohibit you from getting the diagnosis, care, and treatments you need and deserve?

I think there are multiple answers to that question, including overloaded scheduling; stricter administrative oversight; legal and financial risk mitigation; heavy-handed pharmaceutical incentives; complicated and ever-changing insurance requirements; and a growing arena of specialized fields of medicine leading to an abundance of referrals, which can then result in confusing and fragmented diagnoses and care. All of these challenges certainly exist, and they're all making your physician visits increasingly difficult and stressful. That said, there seems to be one challenge that stands out to me. I believe it's at the root of most of the dysfunction being experienced today in physician-patient relationships. Therefore, it's the challenge I'm going to focus on here. It's something commonly referred to as the *standard of care.*

Standard of Care

Let's look at one definition for *standard of care*, which can be linked to from the ncbi.nlm.nih.gov website:

"The standard of care is the benchmark that determines whether professional obligations to patients have been met. Failure to meet the standard of care is negligence, which can carry significant consequences for clinicians."—NIH Library of Medicine[16]

At first blush, the *standard of care* might seem like it's functioning in a protective capacity for patients. And really, in its highest form, it is. But let's take a deeper look into the *standard of care* by considering an excerpt from another article published on VeryWellHealth.com:

"The healthcare provider only has to meet the test that he provided the care a minimally competent healthcare provider would have done in the same situation and given the same resources. He doesn't have to rise above that standard to be acquitted of malpractice."—VeryWell Health[17]

Are you seeking *"minimally competent care"* when you go to see a physician? What if you have a complicated condition, or a mystery illness like I did? How likely is it that those conditions are going to be understood and treated effectively in a *"minimally competent care"* environment?

---

[16] Donna Vanderpool, "The Standard of Care," NIH National Library of Medicine, July – September 2021, https://www.ncbi.nlm.nih.gov/pmc/articles/PMC8667701/.

[17] Trisha Torrey, "Understanding Standard of Care for Patients," VeryWell Health, March 4, 2020, https.//www.verywellhealth.com/standard-of-care-2615208#:~:text=The%20healthcare%20provider%20only%20has,to%20be%20acquitted%20of%20malpractice.

In today's world, sadly, if you are presenting with an illness that is less than standardly understood, and you need a more comprehensive approach to getting properly diagnosed and treated, then you may have difficulty getting the diagnosis and care you need.

Who gets to decide what *"minimally competent care"* is anyway? Believe it or not, the answer to that question can be a bit nebulous. Contributing to the *standard of care* in any given situation could be federal standards, state standards, industry standards, specialty standards, individual practice standards, and the list goes on. In a legal proceeding, witnesses and past precedent will be presented to make a case for what the *standard of care* should have been in the situation being disputed. But before things even get that far, from the moment you first set foot in your physician's office, there are entities in the background that very well could be influencing your physician's understanding of what the *standard of care* should be in relation to your care. These entities include administrators, insurance companies, attorneys, and accountants, and two of their main objectives are to minimize legal and financial risks.

The standard of care, in its most restrictive form, can bind physicians and underserve patients, ultimately creating frustration on both sides and deteriorating trust in the physician-patient relationship.

Clear Indicators

But there is some good news! Most physicians are kind, caring people. Most are willing to go above and beyond the *standard of care* precedent if there is a *clear indicator* to do so. A clear indicator means that something has presented itself in such a way that it *clearly* indicates a different approach is needed, in which case, your physician will still be compliant with the *standard of care* for doing do.

The definitive word here is "clear." A clear indicator that a different, more comprehensive approach is needed could be in the way your symptoms are presenting, or the ill effects of a standard treatment plan, or your lab work, or imaging. Or, believe it or not, another clear indicator that a more comprehensive approach is needed could be you! If you are collaborating well with your physician, and if both sides are receptive, respectful, and understanding with each other, then *clarity* is established. Clarity in communication with your physician can help you get the comprehensive approach you need and deserve. Therein lies your power!

You can relate to your physician in such a way that, even in today's difficult healthcare environment, the two of you aren't so polarized. You can relate to your physician in such a way that your physician-patient relationship remains healthy and trust is restored.

Below, I've listed thirteen tips to help you improve your physician-patient relationship by improving the way you communicate with your physician. These tips are designed to foster a better connection between you and your physician by adding more clarity to your consultations.

It becomes easier for your physician to put the "practice" back into his or her role of "practicing" medicine when there is a clear indication to do so.

Tips for a Better Physician-Patient Relationship

1. **Stand in Your Power** – Remember, you are the CEO of My Life, Inc. As such, "health and wellness" is just another department in your company. A visit with your physician should be viewed as a meeting with a consultant in a specialized field of expertise. Try to never lose track of that dynamic. You don't want to surrender your power to your physician. You never want to consider yourself as being beneath your physician. You don't want to assume airs or talk over or down to your physician either. Listen. Learn. Receive. While they are more educated in a specialized field of medicine, you are more educated in other things, including the goals, missions, and inner workings of My Life, Inc.

2. **Be Receptive and Respectful** – Expanding on tip 1, when a CEO meets with a consultant who is more fluent in a given subject, the CEO is receptive and respectful during that consultation. In the end, *you* will make the final decisions. That's where your power is exercised. Your physician will educate and advise you about health matters based on their higher learning, expertise, and experience in their field. That's where their power lies. By combining tip 1, "Stand in your power" with tip 2, "Be receptive and respectful," you are setting the best possible tone for receiving the best possible outcome from your physician visits.

3. **Make an Effort** – I know this advice is going to be controversial to some degree, but here it is… Unless you are incapacitated or unable to do so, put on clean clothes, brush your hair into place, and put some effort into your presentation when consulting with your physician. Physicians are at work when they meet with you. They are acting in a professional capacity, so try to meet them at that level if you can. They know you

aren't feeling well. Trust me, your testimony combined with the state of your energy, skin, eyes, vitals, etc., will convey that. But if you come across like you generally don't take care of yourself (outside of being sick, that is), that could potentially work against you, because how you present yourself registers in the receiver's subconscious, and it can affect the way you are being received.

The way you present yourself shouldn't matter during a physician's consultation. It really shouldn't. But because your personal presentation registers at a subconscious level, sometimes it does.

4. **Be Clear and Concise** – Physicians are busy professionals. On average, they're allotted ten minutes to consult with you. Don't distract them by engaging in too much chitchat or overly drawn-out descriptions. Stay cordial, by all means. You can start off your consultation with a polite inquiry (such as asking them about their day, or their summer, or their children, or something along those lines), but then promptly shift back to the subject at hand. Try to keep things professional. Identify your main issue. List your symptoms and concerns. Try to keep your account as brief as you can, while still being complete and concise. Let your physician ask you questions for further clarification. There's an unseen barrier that goes up between physician and patient when a patient is too chatty or all over the place. This could inhibit a proper assessment of your condition. Although your health is a deeply personal matter for you, you're still in a professional setting. Remembering this can help improve your communication and, therefore, your relationship with your physician.

5. **Write It Down** – Consider writing down the specifics of what you want to discuss with your physician, then take those notes with you to your appointment. That way, you will be clearer when discussing your issues, and you won't forget anything. I also suggest taking notes during your consultation. I can't tell you how many times I've walked out of a physician's office confused over what my next step should be. That confusion led to me becoming frustrated and then angry at my physician. Whereas, had I just taken notes during the consultation, my confusion could have been eliminated, and my anger would have never developed. Taking notes keeps both you and your physician on point and eliminates confusion on both sides.

6. **Have Your Medical Records** – Periodically, I recommend requesting printed copies of your medical records, then having those records in hand when going to a new physician. I also recommend presenting your medical records to your new physician with a cover sheet on top, outlining your preexisting conditions along with their prescribed treatment plans. In this way, your new physician doesn't have to do a lot of research and guesswork. Also, one of the most common and contentious conflicts that arises between physicians and their new patients is a change in treatment plan that the patient was responding well to. When a new treatment plan results in the patient feeling worse, there's often defensive posturing on both sides, which doesn't serve anyone. Remember, there are other entities in the background of your consultations (e.g., associations, regulatory boards, administrators, insurance companies, accountants, attorneys, etc.), each conveying to physicians their preferences for the kind of treatments they think you should be receiving. By putting another physician's

diagnosis, opinion, treatments, and notes in front of your new physician at the time of your consultation, you make it easier for them to continue with your preestablished therapies, and easier for them to return to those therapies if a new approach doesn't work as well.

7. **Don't Go Alone** – Taking a friend or family member along with you on your physician consultations, especially when you are discussing a complicated health issue, is a powerful tool for receiving better, more comprehensive care.

   Everyone should have a trusted advocate with them when they're dealing with complicated health matters.

8. **Do Your Research** – For every condition out there, there are multiple studies, treatments, and opinions about the best way to go about treating it. It's humanly impossible for your physician to be aware of all of them. As long as you are non-confrontational and remain receptive and collaborative during your consultations, most physicians are open to you doing your own research and then turning to them for guidance. In fact, demonstrating that you are engaged in your own health and wellness can often improve your relationship with your physician.

9. **Seek Second Opinions** – Any time you are diagnosed with a medical condition, your physician should be discussing various treatment options with you. Your physician visits should always be a collaboration versus a dictation. If you have any confusion or uncertainties about your physician's recommendations, or if your condition is especially complicated, or the treatment being recommended is risky, then don't hesitate to get a

second opinion. Physicians are used to collaborating with other physicians, so unless your physician is especially egotistical (in which case, they might not be the best physician for you), they tend to be open to, and sometimes even relieved by, a second medical opinion. That said, try not to come across as confrontational when letting your physician know that you will be seeking a second opinion. Present it as a fact-finding mission. Always strive to keep your communication with your physician respectful and collaborative.

10. **Go Outside the Group** – If your healthcare provider is part of a medical group (e.g., Greater Gotham City Healthcare), which has general practitioners, specialists, clinics, hospitals, etc. all operating under the same umbrella and/or with a common administrator, then I would recommend that at least some of your specialists (and all second opinions) be from outside of that group. You may initially get some pushback when asking for a referral outside of the group, but you can't be denied that right, so be persistent. In the long run, a recommendation for treatment from a physician outside of your provider's group can take the pressure off your provider to adhere to certain administrative preferences. This helps to ensure that you are getting the level of care you need and deserve. As long as you aren't snarky or threatening about it, these outside referrals can remove conflicts of interest and ultimately improve your relationship with your physician.

11. **Consider Functional Medicine** – Today, within the traditional medical system, you can usually choose a primary provider who is additionally trained in functional medicine. Functional medicine practitioners are trained to take a more holistic approach to your

healthcare needs. Since everything in your body is interconnected, this can be immensely beneficial for your overall good health. If your primary provider is not trained in functional medicine, then consider requesting a referral to a specialist who is. Physicians in specialized fields of medicine can also be additionally trained in functional medicine. However you decide to do it, adding a functional medicine practitioner to your team of healthcare professionals will better serve you.

12. **Consider Alternative Approaches** – You might want to explore some nontraditional alternative approaches to your healthcare (such as energy healing, Reiki, visualization, sound therapy, plant therapy, acupressure, acupuncture, hypnosis, reflexology, etc.). Insurance companies typically won't cover the costs of alternative therapies (although they are increasingly expanding into the alternative fields), but if you're willing to self-pay for these consultations, alternative practices will offer you another perspective into your illness, which you may find helpful, and can then combine with the more traditional approaches.

13. **Consider Changing Physicians** – If you don't feel like you're being properly heard by your physician; if the level of concern or care you are receiving feels off to you; or if you feel brushed off, misdiagnosed, underdiagnosed, misunderstood, or undermined by your physician; then consider changing physicians. You have every right to do that. You're not being wishy-washy by changing physicians. You're not being disrespectful or hurting anyone's feelings either. Having a good relationship with your physician is going to be paramount to your healing process.

Sometimes, changing physicians is necessary. It's choosing to do what's right for you and your ability to remain as healthy and engaged in life as possible.

A Personal Note

Clearly, I'm not a healthcare professional, or a nutritionist, or anything along those lines. Because of that, I went back and forth about including a chapter about health in this book. But what kept circling around for me was: health is such an essential part of the *starting over* process (it was actually the catalyst for my *starting over* journey), that without its inclusion, I don't believe this book would be complete.

I wrote this chapter based on what I learned on my own personal journey to better health, then I tried to include the medical studies and opinions to back everything up. Hopefully, I've been able to put together a chapter that offers you some substantive suggestions, as well as inspires you to be more holistic in your approach to health.

Tending to your body, mind, and spirit is a crucial part of the starting over process. Being able to function holistically will assist you in living your best possible life.

As you seek to make personal changes to improve your health, make sure to run them by your most trusted healthcare professional first. Make sure that your healthcare professional is sympathetic to your unique challenges and is someone you can easily communicate with. Most of the stuff covered in this chapter is fairly basic. That said, we each have our own unique chemistry and circumstances to consider. Play it safe!

Get a trusted healthcare professional on board with you as you embark on your journey to better health. Make sure to start off in the right direction for you!

Okay, let's sum up this chapter…

The WRENS: Putting Them Together

Take steps to stay properly hydrated. Take steps to ensure that you're getting adequate rest. Take time to do the things you enjoy doing (not just the pragmatic stuff), because these activities cause your body to release chemicals that arc important for your overall health. Exercise. Strive to stay active and engaged in life. Take every opportunity to move your body. Don't cut physical corners if you don't have to. Climb those stairs. Walk across the parking lot. Remember, it's a privilege to be able to do so. Strive to keep your mind engaged and stimulated. Take time to enjoy the people and experiences you love because those connections will nourish your spirit. Take care to eat cleaner. Eat a variety of foods with a variety of colors to them. Keep in mind that everything in your environment has an energetic frequency to it, which your personal energy can assimilate and be affected by. Therefore, be picky about the people, places, and things you choose to spend time around.

When turning to a healthcare professional for additional support, don't be overly passive or submissive about it. Stay standing in your power during these consultations. Collaborate with your healthcare professionals versus surrendering to them. Don't be afraid to ask questions. Take notes. Do your own research. There's no shame in seeking to be educated about something you don't fully understand yet. Don't hesitate to get a second opinion if you feel the need to. You always have options, so weigh your options carefully. And finally, consider changing physicians if you don't feel you're being properly heard, diagnosed, treated, or respected.

It's All about Balance

Remember the sweet little wrens—our feathered ambassadors of health? They do a pretty good job at meeting their basic health needs. They instinctively know how to get their proper measures of hydration, rest, and nutrition. They're industrious little creatures, so they get plenty of exercise as well! But the wrens also know how to pause from all their busyness and just sing—not necessarily to communicate a particular message, but just to sing. If you've ever heard a wren singing away, then you know that their songs are melodious and cheerful, and they can lift the spirit of anyone who pauses to listen to them.

Let these little birds serve as a reminder for you to take your pauses in life as well. Remember to enjoy your life. Your joy will lift your energy, and your lifted energy will serve you as you navigate life's challenges, including your health challenges. Your joy will also serve as a powerful force to inspire and lift the spirit of others.

Your life is a gift. You express gratitude for your life by taking care of and enjoying your life. Remember, both care and enjoyment are expressions of gratitude.

Truth

Chapter Twelve

When you are *starting over* again (and I do mean "again," because you've done this before), regardless of how or why you got to this juncture in life, you have embarked on an epic journey! You have stepped onto a road that will eventually lead to some new and exciting opportunities, even if it doesn't feel that way initially. The road ahead may seem daunting at first, as it twists and turns and leads you into the unknown. But you don't have to worry so much about the unknown, do you? You can step forward now with confidence, knowing that you are equipped with the right mindset and life tools to masterfully handle whatever comes your way.

But why stop there? The same mindset and tools that allow you to successfully *start over* again in your life, can aid you in achieving so much more. You have this golden opportunity to reestablish your life so that it functions by a greater measure of your truth.

What is your truth? It's your authenticity, purpose, and sense of fulfillment. It's what that star overhead is trying to lead you to, if you can only summon the courage and audacity to follow it.

Courage and Audacity

And, you will certainly need courage and audacity as you move forward on your *starting over* journey, because as you seek to reestablish yourself with more authenticity, purpose, and a sense fulfillment, you will likely get some pushback from others. So expect it, and don't become overly dismayed or deterred when it happens. You might even notice that certain family members, and perhaps even some of your friends, are conveying a degree of disapproval over your life choices. Some might even be distancing themselves from you.

Why do you suppose that is? After all, it's not like you're doing something horrible, like robbing banks, or embezzling funds, or anything like that.

But in their eyes, you might be doing something far worse. You might be daring to live your life outside of the unspoken rules and restrictions that those family members and friends have lived their entire lives by. You might be reminding them of what they haven't had the opportunity or courage to do. Watching you make life changes could be unsettling for some folks. It might cause them to wonder *How dare you?* or *Who do you think you are?* And the answer to both of those questions is: someone who dares to live their life with more authenticity and purpose.

"In existentialism, authenticity is the degree to which a person's actions are congruent with their values and desires, despite the external pressure to social conformity." —Wikipedia

"People who lack the clarity, courage, or determination to follow their own dreams will often find ways to discourage yours. Live your truth and don't ever stop." —Steve Maraboli

Living by your truth is no small feat, believe me. It takes real courage to stand in your truth and live your life accordingly. You must resolve, here and now, to not allow the judgement, resistance, resentment, rejection, or misguided advice of others to derail you at this pivotal time in your life. Do your best to let these unnecessary personal attacks fall away from you, unheeded, as you continue to stay focused on your best possible future. Refuse to be sabotaged! Keep in mind that...

Whenever you embark on a journey of personal truth, you will discover that some people are meant to come along with you, while others are not. Have faith that the Universe will sort it out for you, and trust in the perfect order of things.

Your Guiding Star

In Chapter One, you were asked to imagine that a star is poised high in the sky above you. Keep visualizing that star because it's your guiding star. It's also your truth. Its purpose is to inspire you and guide you forward towards a more fulfilling life.

A Higher Calling

Your guiding star is also there to lead you to a higher calling, if you choose to engage in one. (It's always going to be your choice.)

A higher calling is a calling to do something that you feel you came into this world to do.

Some people fear a higher calling. They fear that the sacrifices needed to engage in one will be too great for them, or that they won't have the resources or aptitude to succeed at a higher calling. But you never have to worry about those things because, once sought after and engaged in, a higher calling will establish itself within your means, energy level, skill set, particularities, talents, values, and time in life. It will be aligned with your authentic self, which means it will feel somewhat natural to you. A higher calling will challenge you, certainly, like the butterfly is challenged when it's breaking free from its chrysalis. But it won't ask more from you than you are able to give.

You will derive a great sense of satisfaction when you incorporate a higher calling into your life. You can leave this world with a peaceful spirit, knowing that you have accomplished something you came here to do.

One Final Tool

This book offers an assortment of tools for reestablishing your life.

Section One, "Starting Over," introduced tools for shifting your consciousness (very important), so that you are in a better headspace to succeed. It included telling a better story; having a defiant mantra; expressing gratitude; and responding to hope in such a way that your ability to hope remains strong.

Section Two, "Fresh & New," introduced tools for meeting the challenges that come with new beginnings. It included giving yourself permission to grieve for what's been lost; engaging in a *period of discovery*; clearing resistance; and redirecting your time, attention, and energy away from the destructive energy of saboteurs.

Section Three, "Wealthy, Healthy, Authentic & True," has been all about the creation process. Its tools included identifying your conflicts with wealth; engaging your *greater practi-*

calities; and incorporating the WRENS for better health. It also offered some tips for navigating today's complicated healthcare environment (just in case you are also dealing with health issues on your *starting over* journey).

Most of the tools offered up in this book are relatively simple to understand and use. In fact, I'm going to guess that when some of you were flipping through these pages, you had thoughts that ran along the lines of *Well, this isn't so hard* or *I already know this stuff* or *How can something so simple lead to more success in my life?* The secret to the tools' effectiveness lies in combining them. Collectively, they will fortify your constitution and shore up the confidence you need to success-fully reestablish yourself.

That said, I can't set a vision for what that reestablishment should look like. I can't write a book (or a chapter) that defines your truth for you, or tells you what your higher calling is, or reveals what you are meant to be doing next. Only you can know these things. But I can offer you one final tool, which might help you towards those ends.

The Journey of Three Journeys

The *Journey of Three Journeys* is a vision quest of sorts. It's time set aside to journey with your higher power, and, by doing so, connect with your truth and gain a better understanding for what you should be doing next. I like to think of it as walking in the garden and talking with God. You can ask for insight when you are on your *Journey of Three Journeys*. Answers will come to you in the universal language of spirit, which includes images, visions, symbols, signs, occurrences, serendipities, epiphanies, and knowing.

Journeying with your higher power is something you can do any time you feel the need for greater clarity and insight.

Below, I've listed the twelve steps to take to embark on your very own *Journey of Three Journeys*:

The Journey of Three Journeys

1. **Set Aside Time** – Set aside a day when you can be alone and undisturbed.

2. **Journey Alone** – It's important that you journey alone. You're about to engage in a highly personal, sacred communication with your higher power. You don't want any additional influences or agendas in play when doing so.

3. **Pack Your Bags** – As with all journeys, you'll want to take some provisions with you. Your *Journey of Three Journeys* is a day trip, so take what you think you might need during the course of your day. I recommend stocking a backpack with snacks, water, pen, and notebook. You always want to take a pen and notebook with you so that you can journal your experiences and review them later.

4. **Identify Three Locations** – Identify three locations that you can associate with the elements of earth, sky, and water. They should be places that you can visit consecutively in one day. An example of how this might work would be choosing to go to a park that has an elevated area with a view, a lower area with trees and gardens, and another area with a water feature. Places that represent earth might include trees, plants, gardens, farms, rocks, valleys, or caves. Places that rep-

resent sky might include vistas, overhangs, open spaces, or rooftops. Places that represent water might include oceans, lakes, reservoirs, rivers, streams, ponds, pools, or fountains.

5. **Set Your Intention** – With a prayer, call upon your higher power and open your journey. Ask for protection, truth, and guidance. Define what you would like more clarity on. Whenever I do this practice, I use a new notebook for journaling, and I write the subject of my inquiry on the top of the first page in the notebook.

6. **Begin Your Journey** – Grab your keys and backpack. Make sure to have your pen and notebook with you (very important). From this point on, you are on your journey. You are in communion with your higher power. Notice everything that is happening around you. Notice the people around you and their demeanor. Notice the animals that cross your path. Take note of any music you hear. Be aware of your thoughts and feelings. Everything you experience now is part of your journey and a form of communication. As you are able, journal your experiences. It's not unusual to notice a theme developing.

7. **Journey with Earth** – Go to the place that you designated as earth. Earth represents foundations, structure, stability, resources, enterprise, prosperity, fertility, health, and the physical body. Invite earth to join you as you communicate with your higher power. Walk in the place of earth for a time. Experience it. Talk to your higher power there. Ask questions. Notice your thoughts. Notice your feelings. Notice anything special that shows up in your environment. Eventually, find a place to sit in quiet contemplation. Take out your pen

and notebook and journal about your journey. Continue to listen. Observe. Write. Once you feel you have received a full and meaningful message, thank earth for participating, and move on to the next element.

8. **Journey with Water** – Go to the place that you designated as water. Water represents emotions, love, dreams, visions, intuition, premonitions, fears, memories, life, creation, healing, purification, the subconscious, and things that are hidden, and it can be a conduit for spirit. Ask water to join you as you communicate with your higher power. Walk in the place of water for a time. Experience it. Talk to your higher power there. Ask questions. Notice your thoughts. Notice your feelings. Notice anything special that shows up in your environment. Eventually, find a place to sit in quiet contemplation. Take out your pen and notebook and journal about your journey. Continue to listen. Observe. Write. Once you feel you have received a full and meaningful message, thank water for participating and move on to the next element.

9. **Journey with Sky** – Go to the place that you designated as sky. Sky represents intellect, intention, inspiration, idealism, potential, expansion, freedom, destiny, higher aspirations, higher callings, Universal life force, divine communication, and divine order. Invite sky to join you as you communicate with your higher power. Walk in the place of sky for a time. Experience it. Talk to your higher power there. Ask questions. Notice your thoughts. Notice your feelings. Notice anything special that shows up in your environment. Eventually, find a place to sit in quiet contemplation. Take out your pen and notebook and journal about your journey. Continue to listen. Observe. Write. Once you feel you have re-

ceived a full and meaningful message, thank sky for participating and prepare to return home.

10. **Return Home** – Once you have journeyed with all three elements, it's time to return home. Understand that even as you are returning home, you are still journeying. So remain observant and continue to note your experiences. When you are safely back in your home, say another prayer to close the journey.

11. **Journal Your Dreams** – When you go to bed on the first night following your journey, keep your journal next to you so that you can jot down any dream images you recall. Even though your *Journey of Three Journeys* has concluded, your subconscious mind has likely picked up on some things that your conscious mind didn't. These things will reveal themselves in your dreams.

12. **Return to Everyday Life** – The morning after your journey, you will want to fully release the energy of your *Journey of Three Journeys* by having a hearty breakfast to ground you. Focus on everyday tasks for a while. Go out and do something fun with a friend. If you can, be around people. In the days that follow, begin reviewing and studying your journal. There will be answers in there for you.

You might wonder why the element of fire was left out of the *Journey of Three Journeys*. Well, haven't you already gone through the impassioned transformation that fire represents? Didn't you do that when you found the need to *start over* again in your life?

Now is the time to rise out of the fire of transformation, like the phoenix!

The *Journey of three Journeys* is meant to be a calming instrument. It's meant to soothe the fiery turmoil that fear, doubt, and uncertainty have stirred in you. If a fiery message is meant to find its way to you on your journey, it will.

The *Journey of Three Journeys* is a beautiful and powerful way to connect with your higher power to gain guidance in life. That said, if, for some reason, you don't feel comfortable doing it, then don't. Remember, you are seeking to connect with your truth. If journeying doesn't feel right to you, or if it seems a little too foreign or weird to you, then that's your truth at this moment in time. Respect it.

Alternatives

You can always set aside time to pray at your local church, temple, synagogue, or mosque to communicate with your higher power and receive clarity. You can engage in meditation to receive clarity. You can seek clarity while on a meandering walk, or while running, or even in the comfort of your own home. You can read through studies and collect data if that's more in line with your personal truth. Just remember that…

Communicating with your higher power for the sake of clarity is more effective when you designate a special time and place, and then make a special effort to do it.

The *Journey of Three Journeys* is a tool for obtaining clarity, but it's not the only tool.

It's a Wrap

In the final section of this book, "It's a Wrap," you will find that all the italicized concepts you've been seeing throughout this book have been gathered and presented again as notes under their appropriate chapters. This was done so that you can quickly locate a subject you are interested in and reread its key concepts, without having to comb through the entire book again.

You might even choose to write down some of these key concepts and work on them as you go about your day. For example: let's say that you're not moving forward with a project as efficiently as you think you should be; then you might want to review and carry with you some of the key concepts covered in Chapter Seven, "Resistance." Or let's say that you're experiencing sadness over something you've had to leave behind in life; then you might want to carry with you some of the reassurances from Chapter Five, "Seasons." Or maybe you want to start your own business, or change career paths; then you might want to review and carry with you some notes from "The Six Practicalities for Success," covered in Chapter Ten, "Practicalities." I think you will find that at different times in your life, certain chapters in this book will stand out more than others, because those chapters will be more relevant to your current situation.

It is my sincere hope that this book has served you in some positive way. I hope it has inspired you to be more optimistic and excited about your future, and that you go on to live your best possible life!

Look, you are brilliant! You are a human being, and your ancestors successfully navigated the Stone Age, Ice Age, Bronze Age, Iron Age, and Dark Ages. They ushered in the Renaissance, Industrial Revolution, Information Age, and Digital Age. They came through catastrophic Earth changes, plagues, pestilence, famines, and droughts. They came through changing social constructs, wars, oppression, suppression, and economic depressions. Human beings have endured hostile and arduous times here on planet Earth. Yet here you are. You are alive today because your ancestors walked through the best and worst of times, and they passed their aptitude for brilliantly figuring things out on to you. Think about that for a moment. You have the same human DNA as the inventors, researchers, explorers, and scientists who figured out how to successfully send a man to the moon, replace a defective heart, and invent a car that safely drives itself!

With the right knowledge, tools, and intensions, anything that's possible is possible for you, because you are designed that way. Your brain is designed that way. So, *starting over* again in life—hitting the reset button at a later stage in life— *"So FN What!"* Seriously, *"So FN What!"* You can do this! I know you can do this!

Starting today, with the resources you already have, you can reboot your life—successfully, authentically, and with a greater sense of purpose!

Section Four:
It's a Wrap

Notes

Notes for Starting Over

Chapter One

This starting over adventure—this quest, if you will—can be envisioned as a new and curious road stretching out ahead of you into the unknown.

You will come to look back at this moment with great pride, because you're going to accomplish so much more than you think you can in this moment.

Somewhere in the depths of your being, you wanted your contribution to this world to rise to a new level. That's what this time is all about. That's the call of the quest.

You never want to settle too much on becoming too settled, because when you do, it becomes far too easy to slip into complacency. That's when you limit your ability to fully experience life.

Once you are able shift into a consciousness of empowerment, versus a consciousness of fear and defeatism, then, given time, all change (even dreaded change) tends to realign into a more perfect order.

If your life isn't growing and expanding, then either you're going to get the itch to change things, or the Universe is going to change things for you, or you're going to start to decline. There really are no other options.

Negative mindsets have no place in this pivotal time in your life. You need to resolve, here and now, to shut them down and tune them out so that you can move forward with your God-given agenda and no one else's.

People of all ages who bravely rise to the challenge of starting over, and are doing it well, are the ones leading rich and rewarding lives. They are the ones inspiring the rest of us and contributing to the greater good in our world, often in ways they never thought possible.

Starting over is always an opportunity to realign your life with more authenticity and purpose.

Every time you start over in life, you have an opportunity to better harmonize what you do with who you are.

Notes for Stories

Chapter Two

Stories are sacred. They are existential in nature.

As an individual, you were born either here or there; you developed this way or that; you've been challenged and shaped; you've loved, created, served, lost, mourned, struggled, overcome, failed, and triumphed. It all comes together and shifts like a living kaleidoscope until, in the end, you have your story.

You won't always have control over what happens to or around you, but you will have control over how you respond, thus reclaiming power over your personal story.

I'm not talking about lying or pretending here. I'm talking about recasting yourself so that, starting today, you begin telling a better story about your life.

As long as you have self-awareness, you have an ability to tell a better story about your life and who you are in it, even in the grip of unfortunate circumstances. That's powerful stuff!

Once you begin telling a better story, and once you step into better roles for yourself, your energy shifts and life shifts with you. Circumstances start to change. The Universe begins to realign to support your new story because the Universe ultimately follows your direction.

You are far from powerless when it comes to your personal story because you always have choices. It's your choices that make you the ultimate narrator of your life.

Make no mistake, when you are starting over in life, particularly when you are aspiring to create something authentic and true for yourself, you will have to tap into your defiant nature to make it happen.

In order to live up to your potential, you can't pay too much heed to your limited thinking or the limited thinking of others. Dare to be defiant! Have a defiant mantra! Have the audacity to tell a better story, then step into that better role! Live that better life!

Notes for Gratitude

Chapter Three

When you are starting over in life, I can think of no better way to begin your journey than by consciously shifting into an attitude of gratitude. Regardless of your circumstances, there is always something to be grateful for—ALWAYS!

When you shift your attention away from your struggles long enough to identify and give thanks for your blessings, you change your brain's chemistry, you change your body's chemistry, and you change your relationship with life itself.

While heartfelt gratitude is a pathway to a more harmonious relationship with the Universe, resentment and the lack of gratitude are pathways to a more conflicted relationship with the Universe.

Graciousness begets optimism, and optimism is very attractive. It attracts more opportunities to you.

Better opportunities seem to materialize out of thin air after you've sustained a state of genuine gratitude.

Anyone, anytime, can enhance any aspect of their life by shifting into a state of gratitude. Gratitude changes things for the better the moment it's engaged.

Regardless of what you are going through, you can always improve your personal energy, as well as your circumstances, by recognizing and giving thanks for your blessings.

It is really through a combination of acknowledgement, enjoyment, and care that you demonstrate to the Universe you are truly grateful.

Make no mistake, we are each in a personal relationship with the Universe. Therefore, remember to nurture that relationship by acknowledging, enjoying, and caring for her gifts.

Everything is changing. People, places, and situations are passing in and out of your life, whether you want them to or not. All of this takes its toll on your heart and mind. Nevertheless, you are still the narrator of your own life, because it's what you choose to focus on that ultimately defines you.

You may have to overcome any number of hardships and losses as you seek to rebuild your life. Remembering to express gratitude is yet another tool you can use to get through the more challenging times. Once engaged, gratitude changes the reality of things for the better.

Notes for Hope

Chapter Four

Hope is indeed a light and airy spirit that rests within each of us, awaiting its moment to rise. Hope offers us no burden to bear because its purpose in our lives is to lift our mood and lighten our burdens.

There is another aspect to hope, however, that's worth noting: you're not always going to feel it. Sometimes, that thing with feathers seems to up and fly away.

Hope ebbs and wanes as circumstances shift and change. Regardless, we must remain committed to moving forward in our lives.

You are, in fact, in a relationship with hope. And just as in all relationships, you strengthen that relationship by responding to it.

You are in a symbiotic relationship with hope. As hope succeeds at getting you to try new things, you move forward in your life, thus fulfilling the purpose of hope!

In order to keep active hope alive and engaged in your life, you should be willing to offer it at least one (if not all) of three responses: consideration, planning, and action.

When you act on hope, you powerfully reinforce your capacity for future hope.

Waning hope requires endurance, even as active hope falters.

During times of waning hope, it helps to think of your plans like a navigational system. They are there for you to rely on when you can no longer find your way.

In order to keep hope alive and capable of inspiring you throughout your life, your response to false hope should always be to "return to the drawing board."

When you run up against false hope, sometimes throwing in the towel and licking your wounds is inevitable. But if you can at least "return to the drawing board" long enough to consider what went wrong, then you've continued to respond to hope.

While a wish tends to stop at the wishing well, hope continues with us. Hope encourages us to do things that move us beyond imaginary fancies.

A wish engaged and acted upon becomes hope, whereas hope unacted upon remains but a wish.

No living thing continues well on its journey without some degree of hope. The stories of our lives won't be what they could be if we fail to hope. Without hope, even our bodies fail to thrive. Hope is that important.

Notes for Seasons

Chapter Five

When the Universe calls on you to do something fresh and new with your life, you must be willing to surrender something else to make space for it.

Letting go of old ways, which are neither serving you nor contributing to your personal growth, may cause you to feel a sense of loss for a time; that's normal. But try to keep moving forward anyway. These are life-changing moments that call on you to live a more purposeful life.

Continue to live, create, and build your new life, even as beloved memories tug at your heart and beg you to look back for a time. Your past is best honored when it's a part of a continuously and fully lived life.

When you live your life in such a way that you truly love and connect with others, then, sooner or later, you're going to experience grief, because all things change, and all things pass.

Love, once experienced, is eternal, and connection is how you fully experience your life.

Grief becomes foundational in your life because your love for what has passed is foundational.

As grief lays itself down and spreads itself out into the foundation of your being, you must get to the point where you are willing to live, love, and participate in life again, even with grief. It's the new life you are willing to live that eventually softens the edges of your grief. It is the new life you are willing to live that celebrates and honors those who are no longer with you.

If everything you love becomes foundational to who you are, then it's perfectly acceptable that you continue honoring who and what you love for your entire life.

It's your continued living, loving, and remembering that continues to animate and breathe life into everyone and everything you have ever loved.

Whether it's loved ones in spirit, or a past career, or a house, or even a special moment in time, try to find ways to bring something from your beloved past into your present days. In this way, everyone and everything you have ever loved remains a living part of who you are today.

Love is a powerful thing. Love is a living thing. True love isn't attached to any one thing or moment in your past. True love lives in you. By fully living your life today, you continue to honor the loves from your past and allow them to continue expressing themselves through you.

When you find yourself in the void, you find yourself immersed in a feeling of detachment. There's an emptiness to the void—a stillness. The void is definitely a place where you exist alone for a time. Other people may be around you, physically, and you may go through the motions of everyday life, but you will feel somewhat isolated and detached, nonetheless.

The purpose of the void is to bring you to a pause, so that you can consider and adjust to a life change. The void calls on you to do a life review of sorts, so that you can make important decisions about your life going forward.

You feel isolated in the void because your path forward is something only you can choose. You feel a bit outside of time and space in the void because what "has been" is slipping away, and what "will be" has yet to be established.

The void is a pause in life on the cusp of change. Just the fact that you are in it means that change is beckoning. It means that you are being given a say in your future's direction. That's a powerful moment! That's a sacred moment.

When joy and love come into your life, they come with loss in tow. Go ahead and enjoy and love anyway. Because it will be all the seasons in your life, collectively, that weave themselves into the tapestry of your life, making it a rich, intricate, and profoundly beautiful thing. Dare to live such a beautiful life.

Notes for Discoveries

Chapter Six

Once approached with the right mindset, change is almost always tied to some higher calling, which, on some level, your spirit wants you to engage in.

New environments beg you to shed self-imposed restrictions and old aspects of yourself that may not be serving you anymore.

You're not expected to have everything figured out from the get-go, but you are expected to keep moving forward in your life and experiment a little as you find your new way in a new world.

Experimentation is a tool that's going to help you discover who you are in today's reality, as well as what you want to be doing in the next chapter of your life.

You've changed. The world has changed. It only makes sense that some of your choices will change as well.

When you come to the end of your life's journey, unrealized potential isn't going to matter as much as what you've actually done and experienced.

Looking under rocks can help you identify what you want to do next and clarify the legacy you want to leave behind.

There's no shame in taking missteps when you are seeking to reestablish yourself, but there is a directive: take the time you need to discover where your talents lie and what gives you a greater sense of fulfillment, then put your energy there.

Not only do you deserve to be in situations that fit you better, energetically, but it's the only way you're going to thrive.

"Harmonizing what you do with who you are" is a cornerstone in successful living. It invites more synergy into your life, which enables you to live your most productive life.

Did you know you were born with a sensitivity that is always seeking to alert you to what fits with your energy and what doesn't?

It's going to be through your feelings of right or wrong (in any given situation) that you will come to discover the right paths for you.

You already know your emotions reflect your feelings, but did you know your body reflects your feelings as well? Your body has something important to say about the situations you are in and how they resonate with you, energetically.

Think of your sensitivity as a compass and your feelings as its points. Together, they guide you this way and that until you arrive at your best fit.

When you overreact, your sensitivity isn't the problem. Your reaction is the problem. Although it's often appropriate to temper your reactions and explore the truth of a situation be-

fore issuing a knee-jerk response, you should never seek to stifle your sensitivity.

Your sensitivity is an indicator of what's going on around you and how it's affecting you. You will absolutely need that input if you're going to build the most fulfilling life for yourself.

You may need to develop better interpretational and reactionary skills when it comes to managing your feelings, but you shouldn't seek to disconnect from them.

Your sensitivity is a gift that, once understood and managed well, will serve you your entire life.

Grace, as I'm referring to it here, is a fluidity in life—it's a flow. You achieve a graceful life when you make choices that better align with who you are.

You move into a more graceful life when you make more personally authentic choices.

Even small changes, where and when you can make them, can have a profoundly positive effect on your life. They are still tangible steps in better "harmonizing what you do with who you are."

When your concept of strength no longer serves you, when it wears you down and chips away at your constitution instead, then it's failing you. That's when your sensitivity needs to be engaged—big time! That's when you need to look for ways to realign your life with more authenticity and grace.

Make no mistake, your sensitivity is instinctive and aligned with the natural order of things. It is an instrument of guidance in your life.

Your joy will fuel your vital life force and become a part of who you are as a soul—if you allow it to.

Notes for Resistance

Chapter Seven

This feeling of being stuck, this immobilization, is a type of resistance, and we all experience it from time to time.

The part of you that is resisting is the part that fears letting go. Life may not have been perfect the way it was, but at least you understood who you were and how things worked.

Starting over is a call to change, and, even in the best of circumstances, that call can trigger resistance.

We are most satisfied when our spirits are satiated, and, more often than not, it's at a spiritual level that we are being called to change.

Regardless of the circumstances that bring you to it, starting over is always an opportunity to create a more authentic and purposeful life for yourself, especially when you make it your intention to do so.

Resistance, as it relates to starting over, is a disinclination to act when you should be moving your life forward in some way.

Good resistance isn't there to stop you. It's there to strengthen you as you move through it and forward with your life.

By taking on challenging resistance and pushing through it, you not only go on to achieve important goals in life, but aspects of your character improve. Your ability to focus sharpens. Your resolve for setting and achieving future goals strengthens.

Pushing through challenging resistance not only takes you to the top of your proverbial mountain and changes your perspective of the world, but you then get to carry that accomplishment and expanded view with you wherever you go.

Intuitive resistance is slowing you down for a reason. It's trying to bring something important to your attention. Intuitive resistance is another type of good resistance because it's communication from your higher self. It's asking you to look into a situation more thoroughly.

Debilitating resistance is a common and particularly tenacious type of resistance that immobilizes you. It often seems irrational. The key to managing it is to first recognize it for what it is, and then to take steps to weaken its hold over you. Once you can do that, then you can push through it, just as you would with any other type of good resistance.

There's a technique you can apply to break through your resistance to the techniques you can apply to break through resistance! It's something I like to refer to as "clearing space."

By taking certain actions to clear space, you can begin to clear the thick, sticky energy of resistance that might be attached to your physical environment.

When you clear space, by changing something about your space, you introduce a new vibe into that space. That new energy will begin to displace some of the old, stale energy of resistance.

Clearing space, by changing something about your space, can be fun to do! It gets your creative juices flowing. Active, creative energy reduces resistance!

You can clear the old, stale energy of resistance from your space by cleaning your space because, as you clean, you address the stuff that old, stale energy is attached to.

Clearing space (by cleaning and/or changing something about your space) not only affects your environment, it also affects your mind.

Clearing space (by cleaning and/or changing something about your space) not only affects your environment, it also affects your emotions.

Whenever you clear space, you can intend for the new energy coming into that space to be more conducive to your goals.

One of the beautiful things about clearing space is that you don't have to address the whole of your resistance head-on to work up some momentum for pushing through it.

Numerous cultures and religions from around the world and throughout history have used some form of smudging to clear and sanctify space.

When an animal acts as your totem, it has an important message for you. That message is often associated with the unique characteristics of the animal itself.

The butterfly promises that, if you can cast off your old ways, and if you can push through the tenacious resistance of your chrysalis, then you will emerge with new wings and a higher calling in life.

You too will serve your world better once you let go of old ways and rise to a higher calling.

When we can meet the challenge of our resistance and go on to achieve our greater aspirations in life, we develop the skills and confidence we need to sustain those achievements.

When you seek to live a life of relevance and purpose, then you must expect your challenges with resistance to be a life-long dynamic.

Notes for Saboteurs

Chapter Eight

The saboteur is someone who is deliberate, manipulative, and experienced in their attempts to undermine you.

Forewarned is forearmed.

Like a moth to a flame, saboteurs are attracted to the vulnerability of those trying to improve their lives.

You have every right, and indeed a responsibility, to shut down saboteurs and their disruptive behaviors so that you can continue doing what you're meant to be doing with your life.

While all of us have our difficult moments to contend with, and all of us can make life difficult for others at times, not all of us predictably rise to the level of sabotage. Saboteurs do.

The sooner you can recognize that you are dealing with a saboteur, the sooner you can take certain actions to mitigate their potentially damaging effects in your life.

A true saboteur will always and predictably resort to sabotage. It's their learned path to power.

Saboteurs don't believe their truth is good enough. That's why they resort to lies, trickery, interference, guilting, shaming, and other forms of manipulation to get what they want in life.

When a saboteur resorts to sabotage, it's a manipulative means to rise above others so that they can feel more accomplished in themselves.

Eventually, a saboteur doesn't just have a latent belief that he or she is, deep down, inadequate, but that belief gets compounded with repressed guilt.

Saboteurs are wounded people who deserve compassion. That said, they don't have a right to exercise their destructive behavior in your life.

Your desire to improve your life can trigger a saboteur.

What you put your attention and actions into ultimately decides your fate in life.

The greatest power saboteurs wield is their ability to pull you off your better trajectory in life and occupy your time and attention with the contentions they create.

Saboteurs thrive in contentious environments. When their disruptive tactics are not reciprocated in the manner they've become accustomed to, they tend to move on to someone or something else.

If you can sidestep a saboteur's distraction, which is not serving you, and refocus your attention on a task that better serves you, then you will continue to move closer to your long-term goals.

Don't give saboteurs your emotional energy. Reduce your time spent with them so that you reduce their opportunities to disrupt your life.

There may be times when you will have to contend with a saboteur by exposing their activity and clarifying the reality of events. When you do, remain factual, calm, and brief. Don't let your emotions contribute to the problem. Let the saboteur's actions and reactions be the focal point.

Keep actively pursuing your goals in life, but remain mysterious about them for a while! Don't share too much. This strategy will protect your energy as you move forward with your projects.

Remain friendly. Remain helpful. Stay engaged in life. Remember that saboteurs love to chip away at reputations, so do everything you can to keep yours impeccable.

Sometimes, running up against a saboteur and discovering that others are supporting him or her is a sign. It's the Universe's way of telling you that you are in the wrong place to succeed!

You always come from a place of insecurity when you seek to sabotage others.

If your life is lacking well-being in any of its foundational cornerstones (relationships, health, finances, or personal truth), then you will be lacking an element of support. You will be handicapped at whatever else you try to accomplish. In that respect, you will be sabotaging yourself.

Keep channeling your time and energy into ways to better "harmonize what you do with who you are." Seek out people, places, and things that resonate with your spirit. That should be your ultimate goal right now.

Refusing to get sidetracked from your better future is the only surefire way to win at the games saboteurs play.

Notes for Wealth

Chapter Nine

If the true purpose behind wealth is to provide you with an ability to fully experience life, then wouldn't a truer measure of your wealth be in the realization of a fully experienced life?

When you disassociate from your greater objectives in life—that is, when you put all your attention on wealth itself, at the expense of what wealth should be there to serve in your life—you lose sight of your higher callings. Then you're not fully experiencing your life anymore.

The disassociation from what wealth is meant to serve, as well as the obsessive focus on the accumulation of wealth for wealth's sake, demonstrates a dysfunctional relationship with wealth. And, as in all dysfunctional relationships, some form of abuse usually follows.

Conflicts with wealth can block the healthy flow of wealth, so that wealth then fails to become the tool it's meant to be for serving some greater good.

Chasing wealth reflects a conflict with wealth because it's all-consuming. Wealth doesn't get directed into serving a greater good. Opportunities to fully experience life aren't seized upon because too many areas in life are being underval-

ued (such as health, relationships, family, community, creative expression, ethics, and higher aspirations).

Misers live with a poverty consciousness. The tight grip they hold over their financial resources reflects a conflict with wealth because it doesn't allow a healthy flow (give and take) of wealth. Their wealth is almost exclusively allocated to survival. It's not uncommon for misers (and their dependents) to live in impoverished conditions, even when they have an abundance of financial resources available to them.

Projecting wealth reflects a conflict with wealth because too much effort is spent on projecting illusionary wealth, and not enough on establishing real wealth. Wealth can't serve any greater purpose because it's not really there.

Constantly struggling with wealth reflects a conflict with wealth that is rooted in a limiting belief system. Past difficulties or low self-esteem could be contributing to a jaded belief that lasting wealth is unattainable. People living with this conflict often give up on hopes and dreams that were, in actuality, achievable.

Objection to wealth reflects a conflict with wealth because preexisting prejudices sabotage present opportunities for wealth. People who object to wealth rarely fully experience life, because they are blocking a means (either consciously or subconsciously) for doing so.

If you aren't using your wealth as a tool to fully experience your life, and if your wealth isn't serving you in serving some greater good in your life, then you are missing out on the point of wealth. You are probably living in some form of conflict with your material wealth.

Your conflicts with wealth will start remedying themselves once you remember that wealth is there to serve you in serving some greater good.

Once you can approach your wealth holistically and recognize that financial, physical, and spiritual wellness are all aspects of true wealth, then you can use your wealth to create a truly authentic and purposeful life. That's when wealth sits in its true and proper spirit.

Your willingness to be true to yourself and stay focused on your higher callings in life is how you're going to fundamentally reinforce your sense of self-worth. It's also how you're going to resolve any conflicts you might be having with your wealth, so that wealth can then flow more easily in your life.

The sense of peace and satisfaction you get from fully experiencing your life and serving some greater good is something that becomes a part of you. It paints your soul in such a way—it can't be stripped away.

Notes for Practicalities

Chapter Ten

The Law of Attraction: Stay focused on what you want in life (versus what you don't); envision your most positive future and sustain that vision; feel the essence of what you want as though it has already occurred; step into the role of who you want to be, even if you haven't fully manifested it yet; strive to tell the most positive story about yourself and your life; expect success; and then, if you can sustain these states of being well enough, for long enough, what you desire will be drawn to you.

Like attracts like. What you focus your attention and feelings on, good or bad, you will attract to you.

Highly functioning, successful people not only have an ability to attract opportunities, but they can identify, seize upon, build upon, and sustain those opportunities in ways that ensure lasting success.

Practicalities will lend you reassurance during times of doubt because they are the solid stuff (the brick and mortar) that support your life. Practicalities will serve and support your creative visions as well.

Good old-fashioned wisdom is still wisdom, after all, and redundancy is reaffirming!

Things achieved through common-sense practicalities are (more often than not) substantial in nature. It takes dedication, focus, strategy, labor, organization, skill, endurance, and sometimes blood, sweat, and tears to create a well-functioning, practical life.

People who crave creative expression (like artists, writers, musicians, performers, entertainers, etc.), as well as those seeking to accomplish something extraordinary (like explorers, inventors, entrepreneurs, activists, etc.), often find the practice of practicalities constricting, when all they really want to do is expand.

Creative expression and experimentation with little regard for life's more pragmatic side rarely achieve lasting success. Whereas pragmatic adherence without creative expression and experimentation rarely achieves personal fulfillment.

Greater practicalities incorporate practicalities that are both left- and right-brain inclusive, and are, therefore, more holistic in nature.

Both the creative and pragmatic approaches to life are practical when it comes to fulfilling their specific roles in your life. Greater practicalities integrate both approaches to help you realize your best possible life.

The field of marketing and development is like one big exercise in greater practicalities. It's the perfect arena for blending creative idealism and problem-solving with pragmatic research, planning, and budgeting to achieve ambitious goals.

Let's face it, starting over in life and making a good go of it isn't impossible; it's always possible in some way, shape, or form. But you must have the hope and confidence to aspire to it, and the greater practicalities to pull it off.

The six practicalities for success include: the practicality of leadership; the practicality of living plans; the practicality of understanding your money; the practicality of presentation; the practicality of critical thinking; and the practicality of networking.

The practicality of leadership dictates that you step into a leadership role in your own life. It's a commitment to living your life with more intention.

You don't want to be a mere employee, officer, manager, or even VP in your own life. Because when all is said and done, only you are held accountable for how you lived your life. Therefore, step into your power. Assume your full leadership role. Become the Principal, the CEO of your own life!

The practicality of living plans dictates that anything that is possible, no matter how difficult, can be achieved with the right plan.

Living plans work like all living documents: they are written, directive, and adhered to. But they are also revisited and revised as circumstances, desires, and goals change.

If a good plan is a powerful tool for success, then a good living plan is a superpower.

The practicality of understanding your money dictates that you stay on top of your financial reality. It includes an understanding that only you can ultimately decide how best to save, invest, and spend your financial resources so that you are both secure and fulfilled in life.

Giving up control of your finances doesn't pair well with the practicality of leadership. Understanding your money does.

Only you can truly know what elements you need to have in place to fully experience your life.

By the truest measure of your wealth, you need enough money to fully experience your life, and to continue fully experiencing your life, whatever that means to you.

The better you understand your money, the better your financial decisions will be.

Better money management begins with understanding your money better, and then by doing the math.

Your money diary is a journal that documents and tracks your entire financial reality.

Like attracts like. By creating and maintaining a money diary, you are directing time, attention, and energy into your financial reality, which, given time, will attract a better financial reality to you!

The practicality of presentation dictates that you give care and attention to your physical and environmental presentation, so that these things continue to reflect who you are and how you want to be perceived by the world.

You never want to underestimate the power of your personal presentation because it's always affecting your life, whether you're aware of it or not.

Your authentic self is your truth. Your truth has a unique energy and contribution to make. How you present yourself to the world will either attract or deter things that align with your truth.

Your personal presentation is a part of your message to the world. Stay on track with your message so that you can attract more personally authentic things to you.

The practicality of critical thinking dictates that you understand how cause and effect are affecting your life, so that you might then go on to make better decisions based on that understanding.

Branding is a consistent and repetitive presentation that seeks to define and then strengthen the identity of its subject.

In sales, the most effective branding campaigns have at least four components to them: definition, recognition, emotional triggers, and repetition.

When consumers understand a product; recognize a product; experience positive emotions in relation to a product; and are then exposed to the (now branded) product over and over again, consumers start to desire the product.

When the art of branding is successfully applied, it introduces a positive message about a product into the observer's subconscious. Eventually, an automatic positive response to the product is engaged, whereas a more critical response to that same product is disengaged.

Powerful political organizations, as well as their organizational supporters (including corporations, industries, nonprofits, religious organizations, and large special interest groups of all kinds), have become so skilled at the art of branding, they've raised it to a science!

When political branding (both the positive and negative aspects of it) is successful, it links our sense of identity to an emotionally charged political agenda. Once a manufactured emotionally charged response to an agenda is engaged, critical thinking about that agenda is disengaged.

Once cognitive dissonance is accepted by the brain, it can become a pattern in the brain. When that happens, cognitive dissonance can affect every aspect of a person's life, political or otherwise.

Shutting out the noise by distancing yourself from politically charged venues and opinions allows your brain a respite from political conditioning. By the end of this exercise, you should notice that you are thinking for yourself again and feeling better about life in general.

You don't want to waste your precious mental and emotional energy fighting phantoms or automatically reacting to contrived emotional triggers.

The practicality of networking dictates that you allot the appropriate time, effort, and attention to your relationships, because you understand that successful living and successful relationships are inevitably linked.

When you bring credentials, skill, and dedication to the table, and you are properly networked and connecting well with others, you launch your ambitions into a whole new ballpark of success.

Your network is an investment of personal energy that will eventually return to you multiplied—often when you need it the most.

Networking connects you with others through an exchange of energy. It allows you to serve and be served. It's going to be through your connections that you come to realize your purpose in life. It's going to be through networking that opportunities come your way.

Keep nurturing your social network by putting down and nourishing your social roots! That way, when the ill winds of life blow (and they will blow), your chances for survival will be greatly enhanced because your root system will run deep and strong.

Once our greater practicalities are engaged, we can create a life that not only functions, but is also creative, expressive, and fulfilling. That's the well-rounded approach.

Notes for WRENS

Chapter Eleven

There are basically five needs that must be met so that your body can maintain its natural balance. These five needs are adequate measures of water, rest, exercise, nutrition, and (when needed) support. Or, as the acronym so conveniently sums up, your body requires its WRENS.

By tending to your WRENS today, you can help ensure that the next chapter in your life's story will unfold to be the best it can be.

When your body fails to secure the basics it needs to sustain health, it falls out of its natural order. That's when disorder sets in, and, eventually... disease.

Your body requires proper hydration in order to function optimally, right down to the cellular level.

Fruits and vegetables are inherently high in fluid content. Once consumed, they break down to release their fluids and serve as an additional source of hydration.

It is during times of quality rest that your body, mind, and nervous system have a chance to sort through the wear and tear of everyday life and begin the process of healing, rebalancing, and resetting.

The quality of health you are experiencing today has, in many ways, been affected by the quality of sleep you have or have not been getting.

Quality sleep is too important to your overall health and well-being to simply be dismissed.

Relaxation, like sleep, is a respite from your everyday task-driven life that allows your body and mind to release stored up tension. Relaxation, however, doesn't require your body's complete immobilization and surrender of consciousness. Relaxation is a consciously present experience that can, in fact, be quite active.

If your body has had its adequate measure of rest for healing and rejuvenation purposes, then it must balance that out with renewed animation to remain healthy and engaged in life.

If you think of time as a currency that buys you more opportunities to experience life, then you can think of exercise as a currency that buys you more time.

Each area of your life—body, mind, and spirit—supports and enhances the others. If any one of these areas is compromised, your overall health suffers.

You exercise your body by moving your body.

Exercises for physical suppleness include gentle, fluid motions that encourage your body to maintain its flexibility and preserve its range of motion.

Exercising for strength involves pushing and/or pulling your body against some form of resistance. You need physical strength to maintain your body's mobility and functionality throughout your life.

Exercising for stamina involves moving your body over a set period of time, then extending that movement and/or time frame beyond your comfort level. This helps to increase your endurance level and maintain your available energy needed for doing everyday things with more ease.

Becoming overly inert can lead to a lack of stamina and difficulty doing everyday things.

Our bodies are designed to be stimulated by touch. Massage is a form of healing touch that benefits the entire body.

You exercise your mind by challenging and stimulating your brain.

As comfortable as familiarity is, it can be harmful for your mental health if it limits your potential for mental growth, stimulation, and expansion.

The timing and ratio of light to darkness you experience during a twenty-four-hour period is known as your circadian rhythm. When your circadian rhythm varies too much from what your brain was designed to function by, it can negatively affect your mental health.

You can lose physical function and still work around that to some degree with tools and various compensation techniques. But a mental decline will eventually rob you of your independence.

You exercise your spirit through your connections.

Your spirit is your life spark, your ongoing consciousness, and the essence of who you are.

If you can maintain your connection with love, joy, truth, purpose, nature, and your higher power, then, whatever else you may or may not accomplish in this lifetime, all will be well at your core spiritual self.

Your truth is always good enough!

End-of-life regrets rarely result from one's connection with love, joy, purpose, truth, nature, and a higher power, but rather a disconnection from any one of these things.

Your body attempts to break down everything you ingest, and then utilizes it for energy, growth, function, and cellular turnover. If you fail to give your body the proper nutrition it needs to do these things, then, sooner or later, your health will be compromised. Count on it!

When picking out your food, if you could potentially grow, harvest, gather, hunt, or farm it as it is, then it is probably an acceptable item for clean eating.

Learning to cook clean may be challenging at first, but it is also incredibly rewarding! Once you get the hang of it, you'll be proud of your newfound culinary skills and your meals will be delicious and nutritious!

Your body breaks down all edible food for immediate energy and available nutrients. In that sense, all edible food can seem satisfying in the moment. But in the long term, your ongo-

ing diet will act as either poison or medicine for your overall health.

When you eat something fresh from the land, you get the full measure of flavors, nutrients, and even medicinal properties that come from consuming freshly harvested clean food.

"Eating the rainbow" refers to adding a variety of colors, aromas, and flavors to your meals.

<u>Nutritional Benefits Based on Phytochemicals</u>

- *Red = benefits to heart and blood*
- *Orange and yellow = benefits to eyes, skin, and recovery*
- *Green = benefits to bones and immune system*
- *Blue and purple = benefits to brain*
- *Brown and white = benefits to energy and strength*

Giving thanks for your food puts you in a state of gratitude, and gratitude is a superpower; it has the power to shift energy for the better. Intention is a superpower as well; it has the power to direct energy.

What you do… what you say… what you listen to… what and whom you surround yourself with… these things are absorbed into your energy field and affect you.

No one is immortal. Regardless of how well you try to take care of yourself, you are still susceptible to developing health issues that are beyond your personal ability to manage. That's when you need to look outside of yourself for additional support.

Sometimes, you just need to go see your doctor.

In today's world, sadly, if you are presenting with an illness that is less than standardly understood, and you need a more comprehensive approach to getting properly diagnosed and treated, then you may have difficulty getting the diagnosis and care you need.

The standard of care, in its most restrictive form, can bind physicians and underserve patients, ultimately creating frustration on both sides and deteriorating trust in the physician-patient relationship.

You can relate to your physician in such a way that, even in today's difficult healthcare environment, the two of you aren't so polarized. You can relate to your physician in such a way that your physician-patient relationship remains healthy and trust is restored.

It becomes easier for your physician to put the "practice" back into his or her role of "practicing" medicine when there is a clear indication to do so.

The way you present yourself shouldn't matter during a physician's consultation. It really shouldn't. But because your personal presentation registers at a subconscious level, sometimes it does.

Everyone should have a trusted advocate with them when they're dealing with complicated health matters.

Sometimes, changing physicians is necessary. It's choosing to do what's right for you and your ability to remain as healthy and engaged in life as possible.

Tending to your body, mind, and spirit is a crucial part of the starting over process. Being able to function holistically will assist you in living your best possible life.

Get a trusted healthcare professional on board with you as you embark on your journey to better health. Make sure to start off in the right direction for you!

Your life is a gift. You express gratitude for your life by taking care of and enjoying your life. Remember, both care and enjoyment are expressions of gratitude.

Notes for Truth

Chapter Twelve

What is your truth? It's your authenticity, purpose, and sense of fulfillment. It's what that star overhead is trying to lead you to, if you can only summon the courage and audacity to follow it.

Whenever you embark on a journey of personal truth, you will discover that some people are meant to come along with you, while others are not. Have faith that the Universe will sort it out for you, and trust in the perfect order of things.

A higher calling is a calling to do something that you feel you came into this world to do.

You will derive a great sense of satisfaction when you incorporate a higher calling into your life. You can leave this world with a peaceful spirit, knowing that you have accomplished something you came here to do.

Journeying with your higher power is something you can do any time you feel the need for greater clarity and insight.

Now is the time to rise out of the fire of transformation, like the phoenix!

Communicating with your higher power for the sake of clarity is more effective when you designate a special time and place, and then make a special effort to do it.

Starting today, with the resources you already have, you can reboot your life—successfully, authentically, and with a greater sense of purpose!

Author's Bio

Gail L. Jenkins was born and raised in the Washington, DC metropolitan area, where she lived and worked for the first half of her life. She's had careers in marketing and development, IT, and real estate. In 2010, she moved to Sedona, Arizona, where she worked in the art community and in real estate. Today, she lives in southern Arizona, where she is a licensed real estate agent with Tierra Antiqua Referrals. When not working or writing, she enjoys hiking in the nearby mountains and along the San Pedro River. She also enjoys traveling and is especially fond of exploring the old ruins and ghost towns that dot the Great American Southwest. She currently serves as a volunteer for The San Pedro House.